THE SOURCE OF OUR PRIDE

THE SOURCE OF OUR PRIDE

THE GARRETT, NEELY, AND SULLIVAN FAMILIES

Two Hundred Years of African American History, Beginning in Laurens County, South Carolina

SECOND EDITION

LABRENDA GARRETT-NELSON

Family Tree Press
presented by *Family Tree Magazine*

San Jose   New York   Lincoln   Shanghai

THE SOURCE OF OUR PRIDE

THE GARRETT, NEELY, AND SULLIVAN FAMILIES—Two Hundred Years of African American History, Beginning in Laurens County, South Carolina

Family Tree Press
presented by *Family Tree Magazine*
an imprint of iUniverse.com, Inc.

For information address:
iUniverse.com, Inc.
5220 S 16th, Ste. 200
Lincoln, NE 68512
www.iuniverse.com

ISBN: 0-595-13275-8

Printed in the United States of America

DEDICATION

This is dedicated to my paternal grandparents, Mattie Neely Garrett and Albert Elton Garrett, I, and my daughter, Alexis.

CONTENTS

INTRODUCTION

"Bringing the gifts that my ancestors gave,
I am the dream and the hope of the slave."
Maya Angelou, "Still I Rise"

This is a biographical history of three African American families that are connected through blood ties spanning three centuries. The Garrett, Neely, and Sullivan families first came together in Laurens County, South Carolina during "slavery time." Thus, as is true of most black families in slavery, "only bits and pieces of their individual histories survive, fragmentary clues about who these people were."[1] In this regard, the descendants of Garretts, Neelys, and Sullivans are somewhat fortunate because their forbears retained strong family identities. "That [our] names had their origins with whites…matter[s] little…[for] our names embody a living history."[2] The survival of these families is particularly impressive in light of the world in which the earliest among them lived and flourished.

South Carolina was unique in establishing the legal framework for slavery even before the colony was settled. Four of the lord proprietors of the colony were members of the Royal African Company, the holder of the African slave trade monopoly.[3] The colony, which was "settled relatively late, [possessed] a preponderantly black population and a large number of African imports." [4] Comparatively few slaves were owned in the "Up Country" where Laurens County is located; most slaves were in the coastal belt or "Low Country." [5]

In 1785, nine years after the independence of the United States, the South Carolina General Assembly passed an act establishing Laurens and five other counties.[6] Laurens County was originally inhabited by the Cherokee. The City of Laurens, the county seat, is one of the oldest towns in South Carolina. Laurens County is divided into nine townships, including Sullivan where Hickory Tavern is located (the home of many family members, sometimes referred to on old maps as Tumbling Shoals).

---

[1] *The Black Family in Slavery and Freedom, 1750-1925*, by Herbert G. Gutman, Vintage Books (1928) p. 4.

[2] *Roll, Jordan, Roll*, by Eugene D. Genovese (Vintage Books 1976) p. 446; Genovese went on to write that "[t]he idea that Black People's names today are 'slave names' is true but distressingly twisted, for it overlooks the formidable Black initiative in their creation."

[3] *From Slavery to Freedom* by John Hope Franklin, third edition, Alfred A. Knopf (1967) p. 78.

[4] *Rice and Slaves, Ethnicity and the Slave Trade in Colonial South Carolina* by Daniel C. Littlefield, University of Illinois Press (1991) p. xi.

[5] *South Carolina, A Guide to the Palmetto State*, compiled by Workers of the Writers' Program of the Work Project Administration of South Carolina (1941) Oxford University Press, p. 119.

[6] This paragraph summarizes *"A Brief History of Laurens County,"* a one-page document that was found in the files of the Genealogy Room of the Laurens County Library; no author was noted.

"[C]olonial South Carolians preferred certain African ethnic groups over others as slaves." [7] Merchant Henry Laurens (for whom the county was named) wrote the following to one correspondent: "The slaves from the River Gambia are preferr'd to all others with us save the Gold Coast." [8] In the early years there was a preponderance of slaves identified with Congo-Angola.[9]

"Most Africans enslaved in mainland North America arrived prior to the War For Independence, nearly half coming between 1740 and 1780."[10] "Only 1,562 Africans were brought into South Carolina between 1741 and 1750. Between 1751 and 1760, 18, 889 Africans were imported; from 1761 to 1770, 18,687 slaves were imported, and in the five years between 1771 and 1775, 19,215 Africans survived the passage to Charleston."[11] Between 1804 and 1807, "40,000 were rushed to Charleston in anticipation of the prohibition to begin with 1808."[12]

One could always find a small number of free persons of African descent in South Carolina, a little over 3,000 at the beginning of the 19th century, and nearly 10,000 in 1860.[13] At the same time, "[t]he number of slaves [in Laurens County] grew from 1,919 in 1800 to more than 13,00 in 1860.[14]" Beginning in 1800, the State legislature began to restrict manumissions,[15] culminating in the banning of personal manumissions in 1820. Even before restrictions were enacted, it was a crime to teach a slave to write.[16] Nevertheless, at the time of emancipation "[i]n South Carolina, a majority of the free Negroes could read and write, and perhaps 5% of the slaves."[17]

"South Carolina has always been pointed to as the typical Reconstruction state. It had in 1860, 412,329 Negroes and 291,000 whites."[18] The lawlessness in South Carolina after the Civil War was also typical, as documented by W.E.B. DuBois: "In Edgefield and Laurens Counties, South Carolina, there were organized bands of 'regulators'—armed men who make it their business to traverse these counties and maltreat Negroes,...in many instances, in the most horrible and atrocious manner."[19]

August 22, 1876

We the colored people of Laurens County feel under the necessity of appealing to you. We are under intimidation with our lives in jeopardy every day by men...who are bent upon coercing us to vote for them. We can assure you, sir, that Laurens of 1876 is not Laurens of

---

[7] *Rice and Slaves*, p. 6.

[8] *Rice and Slaves*, p. 8.

[9] *Rice and Slaves*, p. *126.*

[10] *The Black Family in Slavery and Freedom*, p. 169.

[11] *Rice and Slaves*, p. 116.

[12] *Slave Trading In The Old South*, by Frederic Bancroft, University of South Carolina Press (1996) p. 4.

[13] *Black Reconstruction in America, 1860-1880,* by W.E.B. DuBois, Antheneum (1992) p. 383.

[14] Laurens *"History,"* by William "Bill" Cooper, from the Laurens County Web Page, http://www.geocities.com/BourbonStreet/4492/history.htm.

[15] *Free Black Slavemasters in South Carolina, 1790-1860*, by Larry Koger, University of South Carolina Press (1985, 1995) p. 35.

[16] *In The Matter of Color, Race and the American Legal Process, The Colonial Period*, by A. Leon Higginbotham, Jr., Oxford University Press (1978) p. 198, citing the Act of 1717, Statutes at Large of South Carolina, vol. 7, p. 413

[17] *Black Reconstruction*, p. *638.*

[18] *Black Reconstruction*, p. *383*

[19] *Black Reconstruction*, p. 676

1872....For then a Black man and the poor white man could not dare to say who he would cast his ticket for, without being starved, whipped or shot to death...The boast here is that you leading men about Carolina have given up Laurens into their hand. If that be true we see no reason for it as we are as determined now as ever...." (A Petition to Governor Chamberlain Who Was Running For Re-election, South Carolina Archives.)[20]

By 1880, with the exception of African Americans living on the South Carolina Sea Islands, the typical Black man worked as a farm laborer, a sharecropper, or a cash tenant."[21] Moreover, and in addition to passing "one of the most vicious of the Black Codes....[providing] for corporeal punishment, vagrancy and apprenticeship laws,"[22] South Carolina disfranchised African Americans in the 1895 constitution.

A small display case in the Charleston Museum (billed as America's first museum) commemorates Laurens Glass, established by Senator Dial around 1911 and closed in 1996. Laurens Glass specialized in bottles of all kinds, and in 1927, was the only facility of its kind in the State. At one time, Laurens Glass provided the best jobs in town, and many of our family members worked there.

Laurens County has always been proud of its educational achievements. It has one of the highest literacy ratings in South Carolina. Black educators such as Nannie Allison, a Garrett relation, are credited with having contributed to the literacy rating.[23]

Of the 42,094 people in [Laurens] county only 37 were not native born in 1930. Planters and tenants, bank presidents and mill operatives, all are close kin; and their families hark back to the days of pre-Revolutionary Scotch-Irish settlement. The home staying proclivities of Laurens people have persisted through Revolutionary skirmishes, when the Tories were easy to find hereabouts; through hostilities of opposing factions in the secession wrangle; through Confederate excitement, race riots, and wholesale Ku Klux arrests, which included a leading clergyman; through Red Shirt times when the county's vote was eliminated by Republican officials from the Democratic count; and down to the present.[24]

Regulators, disfranchisement, and Red Shirts were among the many obstacles faced by members of the Garrett, Neely, and Sullivan families during the last decades of the 19th century, as they laid the foundation for later generations to produce preachers, visual and performing artists, lawyers and judges, medical doctors, architects, civil servants at all levels of government, new media professionals; union leaders, morticians, elected officials, small business owners, blue collar workers, law enforcement and police officials, engineers, print and broadcast journalists, social workers, educators, business executives, at least one of a published poet, a professional football player, and a composer of popular songs, and scores of other proud African Americans.

---

[20] *Reprinted in The Trouble They Seen: The Story Of Reconstruction In The Words of African Americans,* edited by Dorothy Sterling (DaCapo Press, New York 1994).

[21] *The Black Family in Slavery and Freedom,* p. 442.

[22] *Black Reconstruction,* p. 385.

[23] From *"A Brief History of Laurens County."*

[24] *South Carolina, A Guide to the Palmetto State,* at p. 384.

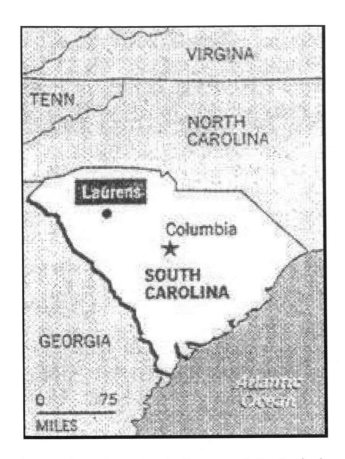

How Information was Gathered for This Book

My family has always been a source of strength and inspiration for me. Putting this book together was a labor of love, intended to document the source of our family pride. In 1979, I visited the National Archives, in Washington, D.C., and obtained census records for certain of our ancestors. At the 1980 Garrett, Neely, Sullivan, reunion in Laurens, S.C., numerous family members completed data sheets, providing information about the names and ages of their parents, spouses, and children. This information was supplemented by information independently gathered by Tony Grayson and Beryl Dakers Burton. Unless otherwise noted, individual entries are based on direct contacts (oral or written) with the individual or a member of that person's immediate family; footnotes are included indicating the source of other information.

Over the years, I continued to seek information about our families, but was re-energized upon meeting the late Ruth Simons Nicholson, who attended the 1986 GNS reunion in Laurens, S.C.; Ruth shared a number of documents with me. Ruth's son, David Nicholson, allowed me to review Ruth's files after her death and gave me copies of additional documents. Ruth's sister, Josephine Wade, filled me in on many other details, and allowed me to review her family bible and to borrow "the Red Book" in which her aunt, Minnic Simons Williams, had gathered information about Josephine's parents and their children. Certain family members prepared shorter written histories (in connection with our family reunions or at my request) and I relied on those documents from: Perry Sullivan, II, Arthuree Neely McCoy, Cora Mason, Mamie Lee Beasley Lynch, and Carolyn Beasley Shortt. Information regarding in-laws was gleaned from wedding invitations and newspaper notices. The history of Bethel Hall was described in the program for the dedication of the Education Wing in 1994, written by Richard Garrett, based on information obtained from Lucius Dakers. I obtained family trees in the form of "descendant charts" prepared by the direct descendants of: Calvin Neely; Haily Sullivan, Henry Neely (the father-in-law of Mary Neely) Willie and Bessie Herron, and Perry Sullivan, I.

I obtained information from the obituaries of Willie Jackson Beasley; Glenn Bolt; Shellie Donaldson Garrett; Lee Pinson; Pearl Roland; Beulah Cora Cleveland; Katie Annette (Wilson) Beasley; Alfonzo Neely; Mary Lee Henderson; Mattie Neely Garrett; Inona McRae, Fletcher Mills Garrett; John Wesley Garrett; Albert Elton Garrett, and Jeffrey Grayson; and thanks to Linda Kumi (who obtained them from her aunt, Ethel Price) those of Murray Lee Neely, Beonia Neely Jeter, Ellington Cortez Moore, Cora Estella Neely, John Ollie Price, James Oliver Price, Sr., Earlye Neely Rogers, Odessa Sullivan Webster, Richard Juan Neely, Smith W. Neely, Sandra Lee Neely Smith, and George Quincy Neely. I also obtained information from gravestones at Bethel Hall, Hopewell, Flat Ruff, and the Beasley family's burial place. Other information and documents were located in the Genealogical Room in the Laurens County Library. I obtained information during the course of many telephone calls (to Lucius Dakers, Beryl Dakers Burton, Levo Oliver, Lillian Maude Townsend; John Dakers; Lnora Grayson; Richard Garrett; Lillie Williams-Tims, Altamease Culver; Bobby Garrett; Paul Garrett; Frances Boston; Mary Clark; Marye Elaine Hunter; the wife of the Rev. Norman Pearson, Larry Woods, and Corie Yeargins) visits (with the Sullivans living in Tampa, Florida, Alma Summers, Lillie Williams-Tims, and Betty McDowell Beasley) and social occasions. Finally, I distributed 70 copies of the first draft of this book at our 1994 GNS reunion, to give as many people as possible a chance to have a say. Later drafts were provided for the review of Betty McDowell Beasley; Mary J. Clark; Lillie Williams-Tims; Thomas Weldon Garrett, Sr.; Tina Garrett; Annette Bland, Alexis Garrett Stodghill; the Rev. Norman Pearson; Amelia Sheard; Marye Elaine Hunter; Albert Elton Garrett, II; Denise Garrett Fredericks; Linda McCoy Kumi; the Rev. David Kennedy; and David Nicholson.

I transmitted copies of the first edition to the Copyright Office of the Library of Congress, the African American Historical Foundation of Laurens County, Bethel Hall Baptist Church in Laurens County, The Laurens County Library, South Carolina Collection, the South Carolina State Archives, in Columbia, S.C., the Schomburg Center for Research in Black Culture, of the New York Public Library, the Family History Library of the Church of Jesus Christ of Latter Day Saints in Utah, and the Permanent Collection of the Avery Research Center for African American History and Culture, College of Charleston. This second edition contains new, corrected, and additional information about our ancestors and family members, the history of Laurens County, South Carolina, and other families that may be related to us. The information in this book regarding Garretts is summarized on my web site at <http://members.aol.com/LaBGarrett/index.html>; a "Garrett, Neely, Sullivan" (or "GNS") web site is maintained by cousin Ray McCoy, and can be found at <www.geocities.com/Hollywood/Picture/5334>.

How to Use This Book to Identify Your Ancestors

This book contains biographical entries for Garretts, Neelys, and Sullivans. Individual names are alphabetized and listed by reference to the family of the parent who is a member of one of the three families. Where the parent is related to more than one of the three families, the individual is listed by reference to paternal lineage (for example, the descendants of the former Beulah Cora Garrett and Richard Neely are listed under "Neelys," and those of Albert Elton Garrett and the former Mattie Neely are listed under "Garretts"). The beginning of each section explains all that we know about our earliest ancestors in America; an alphabetical listing of the direct descendants of those ancestors follows each explanation.

At least two names appear in **bold** in each listing: the first is the particular individual; the second is the name of that person's parent who is descended from one or more of the three families. In cases where both parents are connected to one of the families (for example, where Garretts married Neelys or Neelys married Sullivans) the names of both parents appear in bold. In certain cases, where information was made available about a grandparent but not a parent, the grandparent's name appears in bold.

By looking up the entry for the parent whose name appears in bold, you can identify the grandparent descended from one of the three main families; a grandparent's entry will lead you to your great-grandparents, and so on and so forth. You will also find information regarding the siblings of a parent, grandparent, etc., by continuing to follow the names in bold. A parenthetical following the name of a daughter includes the daughter's married name (or names); however, female family members are listed under the names they actually used (in some cases, maiden names were kept). Where available, information regarding the other side of an individual's family is included in a footnote. An asterisk denotes a deceased family member.

Acknowledgments

Appreciation is extended to the many family members who have been generous with their time and memories, vintage photographs, and invaluable documents: My father, Thomas Weldon Garrett, Sr. (who never tired of my questions) and his wife, Tina (who helped to gather information about family members currently living in Laurens County); My brother, Albert Elton Garrett, II (who checked out cemeteries, spent time with me in the Laurens County Library, and followed up on leads in Laurens); My sister, Denise Garrett Fredericks (for her encouragement and assistance in providing photographs and obtaining information from family members living in New York City); My aunts, Francis Boston, Mary Garrett Thompson, and Lnora Grayson (they answered many questions); My third cousin, Beryl Dakers Burton (who joined the initial search and reviewed census records and other archives); My fourth cousin, David Emanuel Nicholson (who spent time with me in his attic on one of the warmest days in Washington, D.C., and made available his skills as an editor); My third cousin once removed, Josephine Simons Wade (who filled me in on her branch of the Garrett family); My second cousin once removed, Perry Sullivan, II (who reconstructed the "Perry Sullivan, I" family tree); My first cousins, Tony Grayson (who had the foresight to interview our grandmother, Mattie Neely Garrett, and others) and Marye Elaine Hunter (who received many phone calls); My second cousin once removed, Altamease Sullivan Culver (who has wonderful memories); and Lillie Williams-Tims, Founder and President of the African American Historical Society of Laurens, S.C., who has Garrett relations.

Others made significant contributions to this volume before passing on: Arthuree Alberta McCoy (who searched the U.S. census records for descendants of Haily Sullivan) Mattie Neely Garrett (my inspiration) Ellington Cortez Moore (who researched the Neelys) and, especially, Ruth Simons Nicholson (who did extensive genealogical research of Garretts, and discovered documents such as our African ancestor's deed of manumission and the program from the 1934 reunion). A newfound cousin, Lois Yeargin Elmore, added to our store of information about "the African" for this second edition of our family history.

A special thanks to my husband, Paul Nelson, for his patience, as he spent many evenings occupying himself while I was on the telephone with family members or typing away at the computer.

L. G. N.

"This shall be written for the generation to come."
Psalms, 102:18

THE GARRETTS

"The Lord thy God hath chosen thee to be a special people."

The history of the Garretts is fraught with the same gaps in information that bedevil the vast majority of African American families that came out of slavery, although much of our family's history is documented by public records (beyond mere census data). What follows is a partial history of our ancestors in America; it is a start, including documented facts, oral history, and family lore. With time, the gaps may be filled in.

Our earliest, known ancestor in America was an African who, we know, must have been an extraordinary individual because he somehow purchased his own freedom in 1819. The African's Garrett descendants have followed in his footsteps by consistently distinguishing themselves over the generations, beginning with men such as his grandson, Isaac ("Ike") Garrett, who was a property owner soon after the Civil War, and his great-grandsons, Wister Lee ("Wick") Garrett, who was a large landowner, and Casper George ("C.G.") Garrett (whose life was memorialized in published sources detailing his prominence in South Carolina in the early part of the twentieth century). Later generations also produced successful citizens of Laurens County (such as brothers, C.D. and Marion Beasley, whose maternal grandmother (Early) was the daughter of Ike Garrett) of the State of South Carolina (Wick Garrett's great-granddaughter, Abigail Ramona Rogers Harris, was the first African American female appointed to a judgeship on a statewide basis) and of the nation (as detailed in the list of the African's Garrett descendants).

The African

"And God sent me before you to preserve you a posterity in the earth, and to save your lives by a great deliverance." Genesis, 45:7

The African is discussed in *History of the American Negro, South Carolina Edition,* in a biographical note on his great-grandson, C.G. Garrett. In that text, the African is described as a "prince of the blood royal" who was brought to Charleston, South Carolina from Africa but refused to be enslaved! It was also written that he was "a high bred, grand old man who took no insult and suffered no master. He bought land in the early 80's, married a slave woman, built a home, and bought his wife and all his girl children." As related by Josephine Simons Wade, a granddaughter of C.G. Garrett, "Dublin" was the name of this African ancestor; and his daughters married men with the surnames Mills, Garrett, and Hunter. As explained below, the surnames used by the African's descendants may also be the names of the slave owners who held them in bondage (and, in at least one case, fathered children).

Another Source of the Story of the African: Nannie Allison, Family Historian

Certain elements of the account published in *History of the American Negro* are corroborated by a second source, Nannie Allison. Nannie is listed as a participant in a 1933 family reunion program and as the "historian" on a 1934 reunion program (both of which are reproduced below). An interview with Nannie Allison was found in the files of C.G. Garrett's granddaughter, the late Ruth Simons Nicholson. The interview occurred in 1977, when Nannie Allison was quite elderly (she gave her age as 91 in a Dec. 27, 1975, interview, published in the *Chronicle*, a Charleston weekly; she was known as "Miss Nan" to Lucius Dakers, who is himself 85 years old this year, and Frances Boston reported that Allison was the first teacher of her mother, the late Mattie Neely Garrett). Although Nannie was quite consistent in relating the basic oral history, there are some inconsistencies among three interviews that were discovered; her advanced age at the time her words were taken down might account for this. According to the 1977 interview:

"A ship from the Congo Basin, Africa, landed at Charleston, S.C., bringing African slaves. Plantation owners from Laurens County went to Charleston to meet the ship and purchase slaves. Bill Mills and his wife, who owned a plantation between Ora and Barksdale Station in Laurens County, were among the slave buyers. They purchased a slave whose name was Bob Dublin and his wife Nancy. Bob and Nancy had two daughters—Sally and Mary. Sally Dublin had nine children by Bill Mills. One son, Fletcher became a preacher; Zilpher and Marish married brothers by the name of Bolden and lived in Greenville County. Lucy wanted to be a teacher and was sent to school by Bill Mills (maybe Spelman Seminary) and came back and taught in her community. She married Lee Franklin and they had three sons: Stobo, who became a bricklayer; Fate, who was a barber, and the youngest son, George, left home and was never heard from again.

Bill Mills hired Dunklin Davis, who lived in Laurens to come to his plantation and teach his Negro children. It is said that Bill Mills left each one of his Negro children ten acres of land and $10.00.

Bob Dublin was very hardheaded and would not obey. Bill Mills hired an overseer named Clowney. He and Bob did not get along. As a result, Bill Mills sold Bob Dublin to a man by the name of Garrett.

Hunter Garrett was the father of Sam Mills and Casper Garrett. Bob Dublin was their Grandfather." (*Interview with Nannie Allison, historian, at her home in Laurens, S.C., May 10, 1977*).

Geographical and other elements of Nannie Allison's story ring true: Charleston was a slave-trading center, and a 1934 family reunion was held at Flat Ruff Baptist Church, in the same vicinity as that of the plantation referred to in Nannie Allison's account as between Ora and Barksdale stations (about five miles outside the city of Laurens). There is, however, a significant gap in Miss Allison's recollection as she never explained the connection to "Hunters."

The Timing of the African's Arrival in America

If the account of the African *in History of the American Negro* were correct as to dates, and he was in the position to purchase land in the 1780's, is it probable that the African had a granddaughter (as opposed to a great-granddaughter) who was of college age 100 years later (as explained below, around 1881)? It is more likely than not that our ancestor arrived sometime before 1808, because the African slave trade was outlawed by both England and the United States by that year. Further, South Carolina prohibited importations from Africa from 1740 until 1750, and again in 1787, an act that was renewed from time to time until 1803 when it was repealed as unenforceable. While illegal slave importations continued up to the decade before the Civil War, it is questionable whether an obscure Up Country resident such as Bill Mills traveled to Charleston to

Nannie Allison sits in her favorite chair

From The Chronicle, Dec. 27, 1975

make an *illegal* purchase of slaves newly arrived from Africa, particularly because "slavery never became the issue [or the necessity] for Up Country people that it was in the coastal sections." Surviving records, reviewed below, indicate that Dublin was probably born around 1785. All of these factors point to an arrival date sometime during the first decade of the 19th century. It is conceivable, however, that Dublin arrived before the end of the 18th century; because slave traders were not above trafficking in small children, as evidenced by numerous testaments.

In the 1975 *Chronicle* article, Nannie Allison included other details regarding the African. There, she describes Dublin as an "African chieftain" (consistent with C.G.'s account) but she goes on to say that he arrived in Charleston "a short time before the Civil War." For the reasons cited in the preceding paragraph, and in view of Miss Allison's advanced age when this interview occurred, it is fair to assume that

she might have been confused about the timing of Dublin's arrival. Miss Allison also told the *Chronicle* reporter that Dublin was sold to a man named Garrett whose homestead was near Flat Ruff Baptist Church; presumably, she used the church only as a geographical reference point, because, as reported in the program for Flat Ruff's 120th anniversary, the church was not organized until 1868 and the first structure was not built until 1872.

Identification of the African as "Dublin Hunter"

Family lore identifies the African as "Samuel"—not "Bob"—Dublin; however, the only documentation discovered for a free Black named "Dublin" in Laurens County is a deed of manumission for "Dublin Hunter." The confusion surrounding the name of the African is addressed by a letter that was written by the South Carolina Collection Librarian

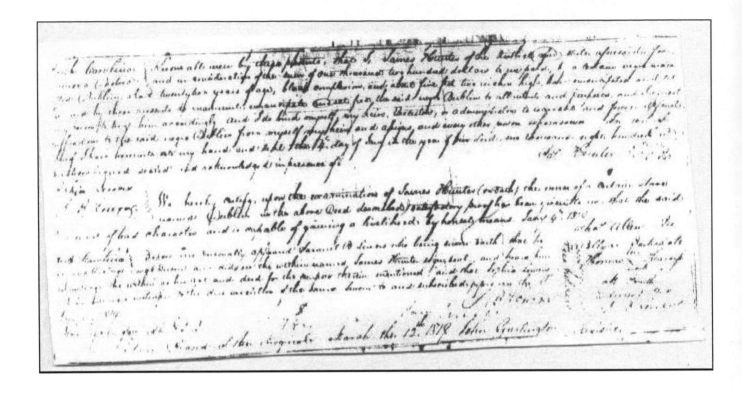

The "Deed of Manumission" that documents our African ancestor's purchase of his freedom
(from Laurens County deed book K, page 239)

of the Laurens County Library (Elaine Martin) in response to an inquiry the late Ruth Simons Nicholson sent to the Laurens Historical Society:

"I talked to several people, and they say that Bob Dublin, Samuel Dublin, and Dublin Hunter are all one and the same. He was brought to Laurens County by one of the Hunters, and he took their name when he became free. Dublin Hunter is listed in the 1850 census of Laurens County as a free man, age 65, with wife, Sally, age 60. Also in the household was a male named Alen [sic], age 14. I could find no land records we have very few bills of sales for slaves in Laurens County. Those we do have are found in the deed books and they are not indexed."

The full text of this letter, as well as other documents can be found in the "Dublin Hunter" file in the Genealogical Room of the Laurens County Library. It is interesting that there are very few bills of sales for slaves in Laurens County; one can assume this means that Laurens County slaves were rarely sold, a factor that could have contributed to the strong sense of kinship exhibited by the Garrett family.

As evidenced by the deed of manumission, a "certain Negro man called Dublin, about twenty two years of age, black complexion" purchased his freedom in Laurens County from James Hunter, for the sum of one thousand two hundred dollars, on January 4, 1819. The deed also states that Dublin is "not of bad character and is capable of gaining a livelihood by honest means." Thus, we can deduce that Dublin must have possessed a skill that enabled him to earn the funds that purchased his freedom. Indeed, as a result of a statute passed by the State assembly in 1800, "slaves were required to be able to

The "Sale Bill" that documents the purchase of slave children by Dublin Hunter, a free man of color

function economically in the society before emancipation would be granted." After 1800, "manumission was legal only when a court of magistrates and freeholders completed an investigation of the capacity of the slave to function as a free person and then endorsed the deed of manumission." In Dublin's case, the "freeholders" who attested to his character were: "Chas. Allen, Collyay(?) Barksdale, M. Smith, Edwd. Mill, and S.B. Lewers." Note the discrepancy between the age given in the 1819 deed of manumission (22) and the age Dublin himself gave to the census taker in 1850 (65). Assuming that Dublin was the best source of his true age, he would have been 34 years old when he purchased his freedom.

The Purchase and Loss of Dublin's Children

The "Dublin Hunter" file also contains a "Sale Bill" (from Laurens County deed book, 66 11-1822) documenting an 1822 purchase by "Dublin Hunter a free man of color" of two slave girls.[25] The "Sale Bill" confirms the published report in *History of the American Negro* that the African bought the freedom of his girl children. The referenced text also informs us that "[t]hrough the treachery of his guardian the old man lost his plantation and the children unbought." In this regard, note that "after 1820, free Blacks who purchased kinfolk…could not emancipate their loved ones without the approval of [both houses of] the State assembly, which seldom granted

---

[25] The first edition of this book erroneously gave the year as 1823.

such manumissions. Consequently, the black slave-holders who normally would have freed their slaves were forced to hold their loved ones as chattel...." Moreover, "once the stigma of chattel was placed upon the heads of their relatives...[there arose] the probability that their loved ones [could] be seized and sold for their debts...." Thus, Nannie Allison's report that some of Dublin's children were slaves is consistent with the report that describes a purchase followed by Dublin's children being "unbought."

U.S. census records also confirm the presence of children in Dublin's household. The 1830 census of "Free Colored Persons" lists two males and two females under the age of 10, and the 1840 census also lists two males under the age of 10. The 1850 census lists Dublin Hunter as a 65-year old male, "mechanic" owning $50 worth of property, and residing with a 60-year old female named Sally and a 14-year old male named Allen. Incidentally, these and later census records tell us that Dublin remained in Laurens County.

The first edition of this book erroneously identified the seven-year old named "Bobb" listed on the Sale Bill as included in Dublin's purchase. Closer inspection of a better copy of the original document indicates that the Sale Bill was issued in the course of the settlement of an estate, and Dublin was only one of several purchasers identified with the slave children who were sold.

There is a discrepancy between the name given for Dublin Hunter's wife in the 1850 census, "Sally," and Nannie Allison's identification of Dublin's wife as "Nancy" (presenting the possibility that he had more than one wife). Likewise, there appears to be a "missing generation" in Nannie Allison's account, as she was not born until 1884, 20 years *after* both Wick and C.G. Garrett, who were reported to be Dublin's great-grandchildren. Lois Yeargin Elmore, a Dublin descendant, was able to shed light on these and other questions.

Lois Elmore (b. May 6, 1933) identified her parents as the former Mariah Franklin and Trayman Yeargin. Mariah Franklin was the daughter of the former Susie Mills and Lee Franklin, and Susie Mills was the daughter of Sally Mills, one of Dublin's Daughters. (Note that Nannie Allison mistakenly identified Lee Franklin as the husband of a Dublin daughter named Lucy; in fact, Franklin was married to one of Dublin's granddaughters). Lois Elmore also explained that Dublin's first wife, the mother of his daughters, Sally and Mary, died. Nancy, the wife listed in the 1850 U.S. census was a second wife, by whom he had five children (including the child from whom Nannie Allison descended). Lois also confirmed our family story that Dublin was a prince, adding that his people were defeated in war and sold into slavery by Africans.

Sally Mills, One of Dublin's Daughter

Nannie's memory of Sally Mills is confirmed by a partial listing of the 1870 U.S. census for Laurens County for a 40-year-old mulatto woman named "Sallie" Mills. The census record lists the following children: Fletcher (a 14-year-old mulatto male); "Zilpha" (a 12-year-old mulatto female); and Susan (a 9-year-old mulatto female). Page 234 of the 1850 census for Laurens County lists a 45-year-old merchant named William Mills (no wife is listed) but, in light of other documentation reviewed above, he would not have been old enough to have been involved in the original purchase of Dublin. In the 1975 *Chronicle* article, Nannie Allison added that "Bill Mills and Sally lived together as man and wife but could not marry because of the miscegenation law. 'He gave her everything but his title.' " The "Dublin Hunter" file in the Laurens County Library includes a note that a William Mills died in 1885 and "Sallie" Mills died in 1901 (referencing Estate Box 273, pk. 4, 1901, G.F. and C.M. Mills).

*Mrs. Mariah Yeargin, granddaughter of
Bill and Sally Mills*

Sally Mills Franklin

The term "mulatto" is defined as a person of mixed ancestry. In a Feb. 10, 1975 interview published in *The Laurens County Advertiser*, Nannie provided additional information that would explain why the census taker identified Sally Mills—reportedly, the daughter of two Africans—as a mulatto. Nannie Allison stated that Dublin was "from a highly Europeanized section of Africa [and] possessed both light skin and a white name."

Lois Elmore reported the names of the daughters of Bill and Sally Mills as Lucy, Sally, Susie, and Zilpher. Regarding the man Nannie Allison identified as the husband of Dublin's granddaughter, Lucy, there is a "Lee Franklin" listed as a "Mills" on the 1934 reunion program, (reproduced below), but—as Lois Elmore explained—he was married to Dublin's granddaughter, Mariah. Lucy married Frank Barksdale, and

taught in the Laurens and Greenville County schools. Sally married a man named Clowney, and they had many children and migrated to New Jersey. Zilpher married M. Perry Bolden, and they had two boys and two girls.

Other details warrant further investigation. For example, If Dublin's granddaughter, Lucy, attended Spellman, it could not have been before 1881, when the Atlanta Female Baptist Seminary (renamed Spellman in 1884) was established—this suggests the continued involvement of Bill Mills with his Black children long after the Civil War ended.

Mariah and Trayman Yeargin were the parents of Lois and Robert Lee Yeargin. Robert Lee Yeargin is the father of a daughter named Sally (who has three children).

The children of Lois Yeargin Elmore

Lois Yeargin Elmore

The former Lois Yeargin married Fletcher Elmore, and their children are Valerie (who married Walter Neely, and is the mother of seven children, including two sets of twins: Sergio, Christopher, LaQuinta, Emmanuel, Elizabeth, Darrell, and Denise); Roney P. Elmore; Angela Elmore Foggie (divorced, the mother of Randall, Timothy, Mareno, and Isaiah); Victor J. (who married Phillis Pearson, and is the father of a daughter named Sydney); Joyce R. Elmore-Anderson (who is the mother of a daughter named Charity); and Temple D.

Harriet Dublin Hunter Garrett

In the 1975 *Laurens County Advertiser*, Nannie revealed the name of a third daughter, "Harriet," who was Nannie Allison's mother. According to Miss

Allison's nieces, this daughter of Dublin was called "Harriet Dublin Garrett." As explained above, it is believed that Harriet was Dublin Hunter's grand-daughter, not a daughter. The article that appears immediately below (from an unidentified text, found in the "Nannie Allison" file in the Genealogical Room of the Laurens County Library) lists direct descendants of Harriet, some of whom still reside in Laurens County.

The grandchildren of Lois Yeargin Elmore

LEAH TRAP'S CHILDREN

by Mary J. Clark and Dorothy J. Richardson

When our Aunt, Miss Nannie Leah Allison died on April 30, 1979, at age 95, she left us a legacy which was the greatest of gifts. It was the story of Leah Trap, our ancestor and therefore the story of our ancestry on our Mother's side of the family.

Granny Leah, a Cherokee Indian, was born in Dunfries, Va., sometime in the middle 1800's. As a child, she was taken from her home by an English slave trader and became a slave in Durham, N. C. There, she had two sons, one of whom was named Aesop. Leah and her sons were eventually brought to Laurens well before the Civil War. They were housed with the Allison family on Stagecoach Road to Augusta, until time for the auction. This stay covered a long period of time during which Leah became a servant to Robert Allison. When she became aware of the pending auction, Leah reached an agreement with Mr. Allison wherein he would purchase her and her sons in return of their complete loyalty and subservience. This was done and Leah's sons were able to grow up together and with their mother.

We are told that Aesop served the Confederate Army during the Civil War as a blacksmith in Charleston. Following the war, he worked for various Laurens County farmers before and after his marriage to Harriet Dublin Garrett. Eventually he became an independent farmer in the Stagecoach Road Area of Laurens County.

Now Harriet Allison died shortly after the birth of her youngest daughter Nannie Leah. So Aesop Allison's children were raised by Aesop and his mother Leah Trap. Aesop and his brother had taken the Allison name following the Civil war as was done by many former slaves, and because "Granny Leah" kept her promise and worked for the Allison family until her death in 1905.

Since Aesop had been so fortunate as to have been taught basic reading, writing, and arithmetic, his children had the advantage of these skills. So each of the males was able to learn and work successfully at a trade. While all of the girls were given the fundamentals of basic education, Nannie Leah went on to finish Benedict College, Columbia. She taught in Laurens County Schools for 32 years until she retired to operate the family farm.

One of Aesop's daughters was named Millie. Now Millie was our Grandmother. She was the mother of eight children. One of her two daughters was Lizzie, our mother. Following in the family tradition, all of Millie's boys were taught a trade which enabled them to earn good livings. The daughters were taught the skills of good housekeeping.

As a young girl Lizzie Hudgens, daughter of Millie Allison Hudgens, was married to Arthur Jackson, son of Jack Nancy Jackson. They were Willie Mae; James; Polly; John Wesley, Dorothy Lee; Arthur, Jr. and Mary Virginia. James died of a drowning accident in Pittsburg, Pa. John Wesley was a career soldier who died serving his country; Arthur, Jr.

was an electrical engineer and worked as a supervisor at Smithsonian until his death in January 1972. Daughter, Polly Jackson Smith, is a retired hospital technician from Walter Reed Army Medical Center, Washington, D. C. Daughters Willie Mae Franks, Dorothy J. Richardson and Mary J. Clark now live on the family home on Stagecoach Road.

Willie Mae Jackson Franks has one son, James Earl, who is employed in the Special Services Agency of the District Government in Washington. She is a housekeeper. Arthur Jr. left two children, Anthony Dewy and Cassandra Elizabeth. Dorothy Lee Jackson Richardson, retired teacher from Laurens District #55 school system, has one son, Airman Gerald Lewis Richardson. Mary Virginia Jackson Clark, Resource teacher for Laurens District #55, is the mother of two children, Lt. Duane Arthur Clark and Alison LaFaye Clark.

We feel proud of our heritage. This story of Leah Trap and others about our ancestors have been told to us all of our lives. We feel that they have helped strengthen our beliefs and our lifestyle. When brothers John Wesley and Arthur Jr. served their country, they did so with the dignity instilled in tales of Aesop's exploits. When Mary Virginia served Army tours of duty in Germany and Africa, these tales went with her. She could more easily appreciate and adjust to the lifestyle of Liberia because of Leah Trap stories.

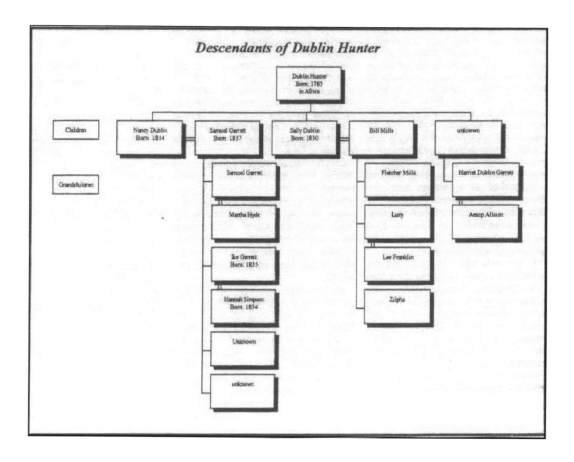

Descendants of Dublin Hunter

The Dublin Clan

Dublin's profound and lasting impact on his progeny is evidenced by the fact that they continued to come together well into the 20th century. The Dublin Clan, as they called themselves, held reunions in 1933 and 1934. C.G. Garrett, who is listed as the organizer of the 1934 reunion, provided greetings from the "Garrett Branch" on that occasion. Josephine Simons Wade remembers that her mother (C.G.'s daughter, Mattie) wrote a poem about Dublin that was read at this reunion. The clan included Mills, Garretts, and Hunters, all of the surnames of the whites who have been identified as holding Dublin in slavery, and in the case of Mills, fathering children. Historically, "slaves often retained surnames identified with early owners, and they and their descendants carried them...from owner to owner."

Although Lois Elmore reported that our "Garrett" branch is descended from "Mary Dublin," the sister of her ancestress, Sally Mills, I did not alter the descendant chart that appears above because it is unclear what changes should be made. It does appear that there is a missing generation in Nannie Allison's account (evidenced, for example, by her memory of Lee Franklin being married to a daughter rather than a granddaughter). Thus, it may be that Ike Garrett's wife was a Dublin granddaughter, not a daughter, or that Ike's mother (who has not been identified) was a Dublin daughter.

We can only speculate about the origin of the name "Dublin." It is an Irish place name, but based on a review of *Book of Irish Names, First, Family, and Place*

Names, it is not an Irish surname. Interestingly, the referenced text explains that the version of "Dublin" that appears in early Latin texts, "Nigra Therma," means "black pool." It would be worthwhile to investigate whether there was a ship by that name. Regarding a possible explanation of why Dublin's descendants called themselves the "Dublin"—as opposed to "Hunter"—clan, West Africans (as Dublin likely was) did not have immediate family names. Thus, our ancestor may have referred to himself only as "Dublin," although he followed the European convention of using a surname when necessary.

Participants in 1933 and 1934 Reunions

In addition to C.G. Garrett, Wick's closest relatives were prominent participants in Dublin Clan reunions held in 1933 and 1934 (Wick had passed away in 1928). The 1933 reunion was held at Bethel Hall Baptist Church; as explained below, Wick provided the land on which this church was built. C.G.'s son, Dr. Colon Hunter Garrett spoke on "clanship," Wick's son, Fletcher Mills Garrett, gave the welcome to the clan, and S.M. Garrett (also referred to as "Samuel" or "Sam" and identified as a first cousin by C.G. and Wick) presented the "Garrett" branch of the family tree. A copy of the program from this reunion was discovered by Lillie Williams-Tims (whose three half-sisters are granddaughters of S.M. Garrett) in the files of Flat Ruff Baptist Church, and donated to the Laurens Public Library.

The 1934 reunion was held at Flat Ruff Baptist Church. On this occasion, Wick's son, John W. Garrett, gave the "response" to the "Welcome to Clan;" son, Fletcher Mills Garrett is listed as the "Chr., Ex. Committee;" the wife of his son Thomas, Lillian Garrett of Tampa, Florida, is listed as giving a short talk, and Crockett Beasley, the husband of Wick's sister Early, is listed as providing a prayer. Also on the program were C.G.'s wife ("Mrs. Anna

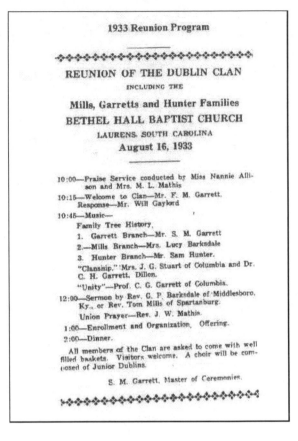

Garrett, Columbia") and his daughter ("Report of the Poet—Mrs. Mattie G. Simons, Washington, D.C.") S.M. Garret (listed as "President"), Lucy Barksdale ("Treasurer"), Lee Franklin (who presented the "Mills" branch of the family tree) and the stepdaughter of Wick's son, Fletcher (Bernice Washington, musician). As noted above, Nannie Allison is listed under officers as the "Historian" of the clan. Thus, there can be little doubt that Wick, his sister, Early, C.G., Lucy Barksdale, Nannie Allison, and S.M. were all descendants of Dublin.

1934 Reunion Program

REUNION OF THE DUBLIN CLAN
Including the Mills, Garretts and Hunter Families
Flat Ruff Baptist Church
August 16, 1934
Laurens, South Carolina

10:00—Praise Service conducted by the Chaplain, Rev.
T. O. Mills, Spartanburg.

10:15—Welcome to Clan—Mrs. Carrie L. Hunter.
Response—Prof. John W. Garrett.

10:45—Music—Junior Dublins.
Greetings from Family Tree:
1—Garrett Branch—Prof. C. G. Garrett.
2—Mills Branch—Bro. Lee Franklin.
3—Hunter Branch—Mrs. Abbie Chappelle,
Abbeville.

12:00—Report of Historian—Miss Nannie Allison.
Report of Poet—Mrs. Mattie G. Simons, Washington, D. C.
Prayer—Bro. Crockett Beasley.

12:30—Sermon—Rev. H. W. Stewart; Alt. Rev. W. R.
Martin. Music.

1:00—Short Talks—Mrs. Lillian Gaylord, Fountain
Inn; Mrs. Lillian Garrett, Tampa, Fla.; Mrs. Anna Garrett, Columbia; and others.
Enrollment, Organization, Offering.

2:00—Dinner. All members of the Clan are asked to
come with well filled baskets.

—OFFICERS—

Mr. S. M. Garrett, Laurens ——————————— President
Mr. S. R. Hunter, Goldville ——————————— Vice-President
Mrs. Mattie L. Mathis, Laurens ——————————— Secretary
Mrs. Lucy Barksdale, Laurens ——————————— Treasurer
Prof. F. M. Garrett, Laurens ——————— Chr. Ex. Committee
Miss Nannie Allison, Laurens ——————————— Historian
Mrs. Mattie G. Simons, Washington, D. C. ——————— Poet
Mrs. Minnie Byrd, Pittsburg, Pa ——————— Clan Reporter
Rev. T. O. Mills, Spartanburg ——————————— Chaplain
Miss Bernie Washington, Laurens ——————————— Musician
Prof. C. G. Garrett, Columbia ——————————— Organizer

A Likely "Dublin" Branch

In the fall of 1997 I began communicating with Gail Dublin, a Florida resident, over the Internet. Gail had traced her "Dublin" relatives to Laurens, S.C., in 1870. She informed me that a few of the Dublins she is related to that were in South Carolina at that time were "Walker" (in Baton Rouge Township, Chester County), "Charles" (Whittemore Township, Darlington County), Maria, Melia, and Richard (Jeffreys Township, Marion County). I became really excited when she related that "according to our survivors George Dublin [her great-great-grandfather] left South Carolina (he was 60 years old in 1870) and migrated to Brunswick PO in Glynn County, George." Also, she related that her grandmother "insisted that Mariah [Gail's great-grandmother] told her that George was free (but his father "hired him out" so he left home and went to work in Georgia as a farm laborer). That is the reason he left South Carolina. His mother and father's marriage was not recognized therefore he had to assume the name of "George Dublin."

Could this be the "George Dublin," described by Nannie Allison as the son of one of our Dublin's daughters, and of whom Nannie Allison said he "left home and was never heard from again?" We know that our Dublin bought the freedom of his girl children, and under South Carolina law any child born to such a daughter would have been free. Also under South Carolina law, a free Black woman could not have married a slave.

I have included below a statement of Gail Dublin's family history that appeared in her family's 1997 Reunion program.

The Hunters

At the 1986 GNS reunion, Ruth Simons Nicholson reported that a member of the Dublin clan served as a legislator during Reconstruction. Among Ruth's files was an excerpt from a history of South Carolina legislators that describes "Alfred Hunter" (b. May 2, 1850) who served in the legislature of South Carolina from 1874-1876. Significantly, it is reported that Alfred Hunter was born "near Ora" and buried in an unmarked grave at *Flat Ruff Baptist Church*—the same geographical area pinpointed by Nannie Allison and the same church where the 1934 reunion was held. The rest of Alfred Hunter's biography, however, sheds little light on the possible connection to the Dublin clan. Ruth might have believed that Alfred Hunter was a relative, however, Lillie Williams-Tims (who also happens to be Alfred Hunter's great-grand-daughter) identified his parents as Caroline and Owen Hunter—names that do not appear in our family records. Further, Lillie could not identify any of the Hunters listed on our 1933 and 1934 reunion programs (Sam Hunter; Mrs. Abbie Chappelle, and Mrs. Carrie L. Hunter).

Regarding the identity of the Dublin clan member who served in a legislature, another possibility is James Mills, who is listed in the 1870 U.S. census as a farmer in Laurens Township, and who served in the S.C. legislature from 1872 until 1874. He married Harriet, and his three children were Turner, Samuel, and Milley R.; the 1880 Agricultural census lists him in Dial Township as the owner of 50 acres, and the Laurens County Deed Books (O at 22-23 and W at 121 &157) evidence his purchases of land on Duncan Creek and Warrior Creek.[26]

[26] *Negro Lawmakers in the South Carolina Legislature, 1868-1902*, Dr. Lawrence C. Bryant, Editor, School of Graduate Studies, South Carolina State College, Orangeburg, S.C., Dr. Lawrence C. Bryant, Publisher, 1968.

Dublin Family History

The earliest records found of the Dublin family can easily be traced back to Laurens County South Carolina. According to an account of relatives passed from previous generations George Dublin (mother's maiden name was Dublin) left South Carolina in the early 1800s (approximately 1829) and became a farm laborer in Glynn County Georgia. George and his wife (Dinah) had three children - Porter, his twin brother, Silas and also a brother whose name was William. The children all moved to Lee County Georgia after the demise of their mother.

Porter married Mariah (no information was available as to the maiden names of the women) Silas's wife's name was Sarah and William's wife's name was Hannah. Silas and Sarah had three children; Lelah, Jordan and Frances. William and Hannah had seven children; Mary Frances, Harriet, Edmund, Amanda, Victoria, Anna and William Jr.. From this branch of the family William Jr. Took a young lady by the name of Alice for his wife. From their union two children were born - Emma and Mamie. Porter and Mariah had four children (that could be traced to their union); Wilson (married Cheney), Porter Jr. (married Mamie), Henry (married Marietta) and Nancy (married Jimmie Andrews). The family lost contact with Wilson and Cheney. Porter Jr. and Mamie reared five children (two mulattos - Booker and Albert Jr.). Johnny, Ruby and Jessie. It is believed that Booker and Albert were children of other Dublin family members. Henry and Marietta had nine children; Sammie, Maggie Bell, Irene, Mary Ethel, Daisy Lee, Cora, John, Rosa Mae and Lillie Bell. Nancy married Jimmie Andrews. From this union four children were born - Jesse, Robert, Willie and Mary Lizzie.

This brief history focuses on the branch of the tree of which we are most familiar and have documented evidence as to the paths that these Dublins have taken. We will take you from the marriage of Porter and Mariah (who were married for over 50 years) to the branches of their tree.

*Porter and Mariah had four children - Wilson, Porter, Henry and Nancy. Wilson's whereabouts became unknown after 1920.

*Porter Jr. married Mamie Dublin and to wit three children were born - Johnny, Jessie, and Ruby (Booker and Albert - both mulattos were reared by Porter and Mamie).

*Henry married Marietta and they had nine children - Sammie, Maggie Bell, Irene, Mary Ethel, Daisy Lee, Cora, John, Rosa Mae and Lillie Bell.

*Nancy married Jimmie Andrews. They had four children - Jesse, Robert, Willie and Mary Lizzie.

Evidence Regarding the White Families that may Have Owned Our Ancestors

Lillie Williams-Tims reported that there was a slave-owning family in the vicinity of Flat Ruff named Hunter (beginning with John Hunter who had a number of sons, including Samuel and Oscar, each of whom went on to own slaves in his own right). The Will of John Hunter, II was found in a privately published book in the Laurens County Library. Interestingly, Hunter bequeathed to his son, Samuel, a track of land "lying on the waters of Warrior Creek" and "butting on lands of Wm. Garrett and Samuel Garrett." Warrior Creek is between Ora and Barksdale Stations, the same locale identified by Nannie Allison. Thus, and because John Hunter had Garretts as neighbors, it is possible that these are the families that owned our ancestors.

Additional information was found in *A History of the Origin and Development of Our Family in America, and a Genealogy of the Descendants of John Hunter II*, by Leon S. Hollingsworth (a copy of which is in the Laurens County Library). Hollingsworth included notes "to illustrate a pattern of relationship between the [Hunter and Mills] families of a day when the area [*viz.*, Scuffletown] was thinly settled." These notes indicate that a Samuel Marvin Hunter married the former Mary Mills, and Samuel's older brother, James, married Mary's sister, Rebecca Mills—two Dublin clan surnames. Further, Mary Mills Hunter was the daughter of William Mills and the former Mary McClintock, and Mary McClintock's niece, Margaret McClintock, married John Hunter II, and was the mother of Samuel Marvin and James Hunter. It is possible that the James Hunter referred to in this text was the same person from whom Dublin purchased his freedom—this James Hunter is listed as under 16 years of age in the 1790 U.S. census.

I posted inquiries on the Internet (on the South Carolina, Slave Listings, and African American message boards in the Genealogy Forum) regarding the identity of the owners of Samuel Garrett. In February 1996, a possible lead was posted by "PMcgee" about a white man named Edward Garrett, who married Anne Owsley and moved from Virginia to Laurens County in the 1750's. A second e-mail was received from "JHutchi427" ("Stan"), who identified himself as a descendant of Edward Garrett, and added that Edward's older brother Silas Garrett, also moved to Laurens County from Virginia around the same time. Edward Garrett was born in 1733 in Virginia, and moved to South Carolina in 1765 or '66. He was buried in Warrior Creek Cemetery in Laurens County in 1794. Two of Edward's sons were William Garrett (b. 1744 in Virginia and also buried in Warrior Creek Cemetery) and John Garrett (Stan's line). Two of John Garrett's sons were born in Laurens but died in Alabama, and one of their sons moved to Georgia. Note that Warrior Creek is also a "Hunter" family landmark.

According to a privately published (White) Garrett family history,[27] at least four Garrett men received Royal Land Grants in what is today Laurens County, before the Revolutionary War. They were of two families and all from the Loudon-Fairfax, Prince Williams Counties section of Virginia. Edward Garrett of Warrior Creek was a brother to Thomas Garrett of Indian River. The "Duncan Creek Garretts" were (assumed to be) brothers, Joseph and John.

I reviewed the S.C. Department of Archives and History alphabetical index, and found four land grants to Edward Garrett in 1770. Interestingly, only one slave document is listed for any Garrett (a bill of sale for a mulatto slave named Sam, "warranted

---

[27] *Ancestors and Descendents of Edward Garrett (1733-94) Laurens County South Carolina*, compiled by Corinne Putnam Mehringer (1955).

sound and healthy"), from William Garrett to Edward H. Trescot, on January 16, 1839).

Samuel and Nancy Garrett

In contrast to Nannie Allison's account, C.G. Garrett's published biography notes that "Samuel" Garrett married Nancy (according to family lore, a daughter of Dublin). C.G. identified Samuel and Nancy Garrett as the parents of his father, Samuel, Jr. Mattie Neely Garrett reported that Wick and C.G. were cousins, and Ruth Simons Nicholson confirmed that they were first cousins (although her family knew the former as "Uncle Wick). Thus, C.G.'s paternal grandparents, Samuel and Nancy, would have been the parents of both Samuel, Jr. and the man identified as Wick's father, Ike Garrett. *History of the American Negro* reported that Samuel's parents were Virginians.

The 1870 U.S. Census for Laurens County lists Samuel Garrett as a 53-year-old mulatto, married to Nancy, a 56-year-old Black woman. Eight children are listed in the household: Deela(?) a 24-year-old mulatto female; John, a 19-year-old Black male; Stobo, a 17-year-old Black male; Hannah, a 14-year-old mulatto female; Jane, a 12-year-old mulatto female; Beauford, a 4-year-old mulatto male; Dublin, a 1 year-old mulatto male; and an indecipherable name listed as a 12-year-old mulatto male. It is unknown whether all of the children listed in the 1870 census were those of Samuel and Nancy. Both 1-year-old Dublin and 4-year-old Beauford were certainly young enough to be grandchildren. Note also that two 12 year-olds are listed. It is more than likely that Samuel and Nancy's household consisted of an extended family. No information was discovered regarding the parents of Wade Garrett and S.M. Garrett, both of whom were claimed as cousins by C.G. and Wick Garrett.

According to the Flat Ruff Baptist Church 120th Anniversary program, Samuel and Nancy Garrett were among the original families that organized the church. Indeed, Nancy Garrett is credited with having named the church "Flat Roof" because of the building's structure and geographic location (the pronunciation changed the spelling over the years to "Flat Ruff).

Samuel Garrett, Jr.

Samuel Garrett, Jr. married Martha Hyde; they were identified by C.G. Garrett as his parents. C.G. also reported that Martha Hyde was brought to South Carolina from Virginia. Lillie Williams-Tims located information indicating that Martha was owned by Samuel Hunter's daughter who was married to a "Reverend Hyde." This information is consistent with an abstract from the 1847 will of Samuel Marvin Hunter, which document refers to a Negro girl named Martha, who was allotted to his daughter, described as "N.A. Hunter also referred to as 'Mrs. Hyde."

Josephine Simons Wade recalls being told that Samuel, Jr. was chased out of South Carolina for the crime of teaching slaves to read and write. An excerpt from an unidentified (published) text states that C.G.'s father joined Sherman's army to escape Morgan's raiders who had marked him for slaughter. An account of Sherman's march through South Carolina confirms that his troops "were joined by fresh thousands of civilians…most of them blacks, and maps of Sherman's progress show that his troops did occupy Laurens County (the map included in Burke Davis's *Sherman's March* (Vintage Books 1980) shows troop movements from Columbia up to Greenville and Spartanburg, and over most of the land area between those cities).

Family Naming Traditions

"Children [of African American slaves] were frequently given the names of blood kin from outside the immediate family; "a significant percentage of slaves

THE SOURCE OF OUR PRIDE

everywhere carried the names of aunts and uncles (sometimes even great-aunts and great-uncles)." Nannie Allison identified a "*Fletcher*" among the sons of Bill Mills and Sally Dublin; presumably, this son would have called himself Fletcher Mills (because he was both owned by and fathered by a Mills). In turn, Wick named his eldest son "*Fletcher Mills*" Garrett. As noted below, Wick also had an uncle named Fletcher Garrett. Wick also named one daughter after his sister, Early, and another after his sister, Hattie.

Fletcher Mills Garrett did not have a son, but 49 years after his birth, his brother, Albert Elton Garrett, continued this family naming tradition by calling one of his sons Bobby *Fletcher* Garrett. Albert Elton Garrett also named other children after relatives: Twins, Wister Pickney (called Paul) and Mary Lee—Paul's given name was a combination of the names of his Garrett and Neely grandfathers, and Mary had the same first name as Wick's sister (and according to Nannie Allison, one of Dublin's daughters); son Thomas was named after a brother; and daughter Frances was named after his mother (Albert Elton's sister, Beulah, also had a granddaughter named after Frances).

Over the generations, the daughters of the Garrett family have consistently included "Garrett" in the names of their children: C.G.'s daughter, Mattie Simons, named a son Casper Garrett Simons, and one of Mattie's daughters named a son William *Garrett* Nicholson. Wick's direct descendants have followed suit: One of Wick's granddaughters named a son Wilfred *Garrett* Rogers, and this same granddaughter's daughter named her daughter *Garrett* Ella Harris; another great-grandson of Wick's is the Reverend Glenn *Garrett* Grayson (who has a son by the same name) and yet another great-granddaughter named her daughter Alexis *Garrett* Stodghill. Similarly, Wick's daughter Beulah Cora (who married a Neely) named a son *Garrett* Neely, and Mamie Kennedy (a daughter of Sam Garrett) named a son *Garrett* Kennedy. C.G.'s granddaughter, Josephine

Simons Wade, recalls a cousin who attended Howard University named *Garrett* Ridgley.

Regarding the Mills and Hunter branches of the Dublin Clan, in addition to Wick's naming of Fletcher *Mills* Garrett, C.G. Garrett named a daughter, Naomi *Mills (who is called "Aunt Mills")* and a son, Colon *Hunter*. C.G.'s daughter, Mattie Simons, named a son *Mills* McDaniel.

A Second Family of African American Garretts in Laurens County

I obtained the family history that appears immediately below from Linda Boyd, a childhood friend whom I have always called "cousin." We have considered ourselves cousins because all of our parents were born in Laurens County, and her mother was born a "Garrett." It does appear that related White Garretts owned us all; in this regard, one of my Internet correspondents from the White Garrett family reported that "the [Garrett] families who would have had slaves prior to the 1860s' were...narrowly located." Thus, it might be that a relationship between this set of Garretts and ours pre-dates our move from Virginia to South Carolina; however, we have yet to pinpoint a direct relationship between our families.

Lois Yeargin Elmore reports that her grandmother (Susie Lee Mills, a Dublin granddaughter) always said that Ed McDaniel's grandmother bore the same relation to her as my Garrett grandfather (Elp Garrett, I). Ed McDaniel's parents were Darling Augustus McDaniel and the former Ethel Taggart; Darling Augustus McDaniel was the son of the former Ida Garrett and Augustus McDaniel; and Ida Garrett was the daughter of the former Mary Casey Franklin and Isam Garrett (Jan. 4, 1852-June 30, 1910, buried at Beaverdam), a son of the slave woman, Ceelie, with whom the history reprinted below begins. I compared the surnames used by Ceelie Garrett's descendants to the unidentified

Garrett Family History

This is an attempt to weave the legacy of our ancestors, beginning with **Ceelie Garrettt.** It does reflect the recollection of **Ozella Garrett Gray** and the recollections of other family members having been passed down by word of mouth. You can help us by sharing your stories with us to make the account more complete. Please pass on any information concerning our family to **Carrie Taylor,** who will include your information in the next installment of the **Garrett Family History.**

Ceelie Garrett had two girls and seven boys. Her two daughters were sold in slavery and taken to Mississippi and never heard from again. Her seven sons, **Willis, Andy, Nathan, Zack, Green, Dick** and **Isam** are listed below along with their offspring.

Laurens County records show two references to Ceelie Garrett. The will of Edward Garrett III (1787-1864), 16th child of Edward and Ann Garrett who migrated to Laurens County from Virginia and settled, recorded one woman Ceelie (spelled Selah) appraised at $300. The acreage of Edward Garrett included some 500 acres between Warrieor Creek and Martin's Crossroads and 31 acres along Beaverdam Creek. The 1870 census records show Ceelie (spelled Cecilia) mother to Andrew head of household in the Youngs section of Laurens County which ran in the same vicinity of the property of Edward Garrett. (Copy of Laurens County map in 1883 is attached).

Official records for Edward Garrett III listed among his property the following who sons of Ceelie: Willis appraised at $1550, Andy appraised at $1700, Nathan appraised at $1700, Green appraised at $1700, Isam appraised at $1250. Records published in Garrett Family (white) geneology in the Laurens County Library and dated January 30, 1858 show the transfer of Negroes by Edward Garrett to members of his family with accounting at the distribution of his estate the following verified family members: Dick appraised at $666, Zack appraised at $830 and Wash appraised at $630 (son of Andrew). Other transfers in this same document but not verified as descendants of Ceelie include: Lacey appraised at $525, Alfred appraised at $600 and Caroline appraised at $680.

Ike Garrett (1835-1911)

The Maternal Grandmother of Ike Garrett's Children, Lucy Simpson

names on the '33 and '34 reunion programs and found no matches. If Lois Yeargin Elmore's report is accurate, there are several possible explanations, including that Ida Garrett was related to Elp Garrett through her mother (Mary), or that our information is simply incomplete.

Ike Garrett

Ike Garrett died at the age of 76, on June 8, 1911 (as shown on his gravestone). Ike was the son of Samuel and Nancy Garrett. Ike married the former Hannah Simpson (whose gravestone indicates that she died on Mar. 2, 1888 at age 54) and they are buried side-by-side at New Grove Baptist Church in Laurens, S.C. In addition to Wick and Early, Ike and Hannah Garrett had seven other children: Lela (Beeks); Hattie (Milan); Dicey (Johnson, then Irby); Jefferson; Tildy (Austin, then Sexton); Mary; and Guy (who left South Carolina and was

never heard from again) The typical occupation listed for African Americans living in Laurens Township at the time of the 1870 U.S. Census was "laborer." Thus, we know that Ike Garrett (whose age is listed as 32 at the time) was atypical, because he is described as a farmer, and Hannah (whose age is listed as 23) is described as a Housekeeper. South Carolina was listed as the birthplace of Ike, his wife, and the four children living in the household ("Dicy, Wick, Jefferson, and Corra"—the last name may be a reference to Early whose middle initial was "C").

Ike Garrett's wife, Hannah, was the daughter of Jim and Lucy Simpson. Lucy Simpson (b.1825, d. Dec. 17, 1914) lived with Wick Garrett until the end of her life, and is buried near him at Bethel Hall Baptist Church, in Hickory Tavern, South Carolina. Given the 1825 birth date on Lucy Simpson's gravestone, it appears that the age Hannah Garrett gave the

1870 census taker (23) was the correct one. The age listed on Hannah's gravestone would suggest that she was born in 1834 (when Lucy was only nine years old) whereas the census record indicates that she was born in 1841, when Lucy would have been 14.

Regarding the "Simpson" surname, I received an e-mail from a descendant of African American Simpsons in Laurens County who believe that the family may have been owned by J. Wister Simpson, and that part of the family was sold to a Gabriel Pinson. This report came from a descendant of Sawney Simpson (born around 1815, died about 1894), whose son was David Simpson (born around 1851). David Simpson's son, Berry Simpson reported that "we were sold to Gabe Pinson but took the name Simpson back after freedom." John Wister Simpson, an attorney, had a Black male slave who was the right age for Sawney, three of his children had the same name as three of Sawney's children 20 years later, and David named one of his sons Wister.

Mary Garrett Thompson discovered Ike Garrett's photograph as well as those of Wick Garrett's eldest daughter, Hattie, what is believed to be a picture of Wick's wife in her youth, and Lucy Simpson in February 1996. In the company of her niece, LaBrenda Garrett-Nelson, and nephew, Albert Elton Garrett, II, Mary retrieved four large picture frames from the last home of her late uncle, John Wesley Garrett. John Wesley was the last of their children to live in the home of Wick and Frances Garrett, and Mary desired the frames because she knew that they had once hung there. The next morning, in the presence of LaBrenda, behind commercial prints that had been placed in the frame, Mary discovered the four photographs and Hattie Garrett's 1908 college degree. All four photographs were very similar in appearance and were the same size. Lucius Dakers, Wick Garrett's nephew and foster child, positively identified the photographs of Hattie and Lucy Simpson. The photograph of Ike Garrett was the only one with writing on the back, but it was Wick Garrett's name that was written. Lucius Dakers does not remember having seen a likeness of Ike Garrett, but he does recall that Wick did possess a large photograph of his father. Lucius could not positively identify Frances's likeness, but Mary Garrett Thompson based her identification on the hairstyle of the woman in the photograph that is believed to be of Frances.

Casper George Garrett

C.G. Garrett (b. Sept. 1865; d. 1948) the son of Samuel Garrett Jr., and the former Martha Hyde, married the former Anna Maria—pronounced "Mariah"—Threewitts on Nov. 26, 1890. Anna Maria (who lived from 1871 until 1944) was the daughter of Anderson Threewitts (1830-1892) and the former Phyllis Peacher (1836-1893). Phyllis Peacher was the daughter of Joseph Peacher, a member of a prominent family of free Blacks who lived in Charleston, S.C., before the Civil War; Joseph Peacher died in Careytown, Liberia. Casper George and Anna had nine children: Ralston Proudfit; Casper, Jr.; Colon Hunter; Maceo Fleming; Marion Threewitts; Christopher Threewitts; Ruth Eider (Butcher); Naomi Mills; Frances (an adopted daughter who was the natural daughter of Ralston Proudfit Garrett); and Mattie Phyllis (Simons).

Few men in South Carolina were more widely known than C.G. Garrett. Josephine Simons Wade recalls that a photograph of C.G. and his wife appeared on the first page of *The State*, on their 50th wedding anniversary. The highlights of C.G.'s career are described in the 1919 South Carolina edition of *History of the American Negro:* After passing the county examination in 1883, he taught for years in the Laurens public schools; he served as principal of the Winnsboro school for four years; after being elected to a professorship there in 1895, he became vice president of Allen University, in Columbia, S.C.; he was the superintendent of the Mayesville

C.G.'s Family in 1901: C.G., Martha Phyllis, Marion, Ruth, Anna Maria, Colon, Ralston, C.G., Jr., and Maceo

Industrial Institute in 1918; he was in the active practice of law for some time (having read law with a white lawyer named Ralston Proudfit, after whom he named one of his sons, and passing an examination before the South Carolina Supreme Court); and, he was an influential journalist (he established "The Light," a weekly newspaper in Columbia, S. C.).

As noted in his biography, all of C.G.'s children were afforded the best educational advantages. Mattie Phyllis Garrett Simons was the first female graduate of the College Department at Allen University; another daughter, Dr. Naomi Mills Garrett, Ph.D., is listed in *Who's Who of American Women* and *Biography of American Scholars*; a son, Dr. Colon Hunter Garrett, was a 1927 graduate of the Meharry Dental School; Marion Threewitts Garrett attended South Carolina State; and Casper Garrett, Jr., as recalled by his niece, Josephine Simons Wade, co-wrote a play with the famous author, Langston Hughes. C.G.'s daughter, Mattie Garrett Simons, settled in Washington, D.C., and her children and grandchildren include Josephine Simons Wade, who taught in the D.C. public school system for 47 years; William Simons, a former president of the Washington, D.C. Teacher's Union; Dr. Alfred Edgar Simons, Ph.D., a professor at Prince George's Community College; David Nicholson, an assistant editor at the *Washington Post*; Dr. Phyllis Nicholson, M.D., a 1982 graduate of the University of Maryland Medical School; Josephine Nicholson, a performing artist, and William Garrett Nicholson, a graduate of the Georgetown University Law Center. Mattie Garrett Simon's daughter, the late Ruth Simons Nicholson, devoted the last years of her life to researching the Garrett family tree, and the family is indebted to her for re-discovering much of our lost past.

November of 1940: C.G.'s 50th anniversary, from foreground: Casper Garrett Simons, Jr. (in lap of) Anna Maria Threewitts Garrett, Josephine Simons Wade (on left) Mattie Garrett Simons, and C.G. (standing)

As noted above, C.G. Garrett's biography appears in several texts, in addition to numerous other contemporary references to his activities. When Booker T. Washington toured South Carolina in March of 1909, C.G. Garrett was listed among the "twenty-four…distinguished and prominent men…" who were in his party. (From the files of Ruth Simons Nicholson, with a note indicating that this report was found in the Booker T. Washington Archives of the Library of Congress).

Wick Garrett

Wick Garrett was born on Aug. 16, 1863, the son of Ike Garrett and the former Hannah Simpson. Although the Civil War ended after Wick's birth (in 1865) the Jan. 1, 1863 effective date of Lincoln's Emancipation Proclamation meant that Wick was born "then, thenceforward, and forever free." (The proclamation only applied to slaves in rebellion against the United States, as South Carolina was on that date.) Wick married the former Frances J. Latimer (b. Apr. 2, 1865, d. Dec. 31, 1953). The photograph that appears on this page is of Wick at the age of 27, in 1890. The couple raised 13 children: Fletcher Mills; Thomas; Beulah Cora (Neely, then Cleveland); Early (Smith); Hattie; Albert Elton; Otto; Cloda; Shellie Donaldson; John Wesley; and Celeste (Coleman)—in addition to two of his sister Dicey's grandchildren: Creselene Dakers and Lucius Dakers—A Wick, Jr. is listed as a three-month old in

PROF. C. G. GARRETT, A.M., LL.D.

From the files of Ruth Simons Nicholson
(with a note indicating that this report was found in
the Booker T. Washington Archives of the
Library of Congress)

DR. BOOKER T. WASHINGTON'S Tour of South Carolina begins March 14, 1909.

The party which will consist of about twenty-four, all distinguished and prominent men will board a special car at Charlotte, N. C. The first stop will be at Rock Hill, S. C., Sunday afternoon, March 14, for a few hours. But short speeches will be made while the train stops at Chester and Winnsboro. On the fifteenth (15) the South Carolina party will join at Columbia and will visit the following towns if the citizens make ample and satifactory arrangements; otherwise the program will be changed; Columbia, Orangeburg, Aiken, Denmark, Sumter, Florence, Georgetown, Charleston, Anderson, Greenville, Spartanburg and Gaffney. Citizens along the line of road which we travel will have the opportunity of seeing Mr. Washington; while the train stops at these places he will make short addresses. It is urged where ever Mr. Washington speaks all the citizens come out as this may be his last visit to South Carolina. We want every town to do its best—to give Mr. Washington a great reception. He is the GREATEST NEGRO IN THE WORLD TODAY and has few superiors in other races. In this party will be:

Dr. R. E. Parks, (white) A News Paper Correspondent of Boston, Mass. Mr. Whitfield McKinley, a prominet bussiness man of Washington, D. C., Mr. Chas. Steward of Chicago. A News Paper Correspondent. Mr. Emmett J. Scott, Secretary Business League of America; Mr. N. Hunt, private secretary to Mr. Washington; Dr. C. T. Walker of August, Ga.; Bishop Lee of Ohio, and others from outside of the state. Among the South Carolina party will be such men as: J. J. Durham, M. D., D. D.; E. D. White, D. D. Secretary of Baptist State Convention; T. A. Williams, Esq. Secretary State Fair Association; P. S. Maloy, D. D., Dr. J. L. Dart, D. D., Editor of the Southern Reporter; Dr. H. W. P. Bennet of Charleston, S. C.; Pastor Emanuel A. M. E. Church; Dr E. B. Burroughs, Pastor Wesley M. E. Church, Charleston; C. C. Johnson, M. D.; Rev. A. G. Kenedy, Mr. C. P. T. White, Editor Rock Hill Messenger; Rev. D. J. Jenkins, Editor Charleston of Messenger; Rev. C. F. Holmes, Prof. C. E. Garrett, Editor The Light, Rev. W. H. Howard, S. S. Missionary; J. R. Levy, M. D., Rev. C. R. Brown, Vice President State Fair Association; J. H. Goodwin, M. D., Hon Z. E. Walker, Supt. State Fair Association; R. W. Westberry, Sect'y State Fair Association; W. T. Andrews, Esq., Member Executive Committee Negro Business League, C. C. Bowman, Business man; Rev. M. M. Mazon, D. D., Pastor Century M. E. Church, Charleston; Richard Carroll and others. The party will travel in a special car attached to the regular train. Arrangements must be made at every place where stops are made to entertain the entire party in the homes of distinguished citizens. All secret orders and other organizations are urged to turn out. The tour begins Mar. 14 and ends Mar. 21 Gaffney. At present the following dates will be observed: Rockhill, Sunday afternoon, Mar. 14, (If possible schedule is made train). Columbia, Monday night, Mar. 15, (Opera House) 8 p. m. Aiken, Tuesday morning, Mar. 16, (11 a. m.) Denmark, Tuesday afternoon, Mar. 16, (5 p. m.) Orangeburg, Wednesday morning, Mar. 17, (11 a. m.) Claflin. Sumter, Thurday morning, Mar. 18, (11 a.) Florence, Thursday night, Mar. 18, (8 p. m.) Georgetown, Friday morning, Mar. 19, (11 a. m.) Charleston, Friday night, Mar. 9, 9. a. m. (one hour late.) Anderson, Saturday noon, Mar. 20. Greenville, Saturday night, Mar. 20, 8 p. m. Spartanburg, Sunday morning, Mar. 21, 11 a. m. Gaffney, Sunday evening, Mar. 21, 4 p. m. These are the cities we will visit if the citizens make proper arrangements. This is the best we can do the present as Mr. Washington's time will be limited. The expenses of the party, will be at least sixty dollars ($60) a day besides local expenses. The special coach must be paid for in advance. We hope that the colored citizens will organize in every town. Should we find that any town mentioned above cannot meet the expenses of the party we will have to change our program. Mr. Washington's party will travel under the auspices of the "SOUTH CAROLINA RACE CONFERENCE".

1986: Ruth Simons Nicholson (holding book) sharing "history" with Tony Grayson and Jackie Garrett (Thomas Weldon Garrett, Jr., to her right)

Hattie Garrett

built a large, two-story, six-to seven-bedroom, frame house, on what is now Boyd's Mill Pond Road in Hickory Tavern. His home was filled with beautiful oak furnishings, and his grandchildren have preserved many of these treasures (Willie Harold Garrett is in possession of the large hall tree; Frances Boston has a superb suite of bedroom furniture; and the oak dining table graces the home of Bobby Garrett). Supervising his workers astride a horse, Wick raised every crop the area would bear (including corn, wheat, and cotton), sold meat from his smoke house, and raised poultry. Wick himself cleared much of his land; indeed, his daughter-in-law, Mattie Neely Garrett, always maintained that he died from hard work. He left about 35 acres to each of his children. About 140 acres remain in family hands (owned in varying proportions by the children and grandchildren of Shellie Donaldson and Albert Elton).

Not much is known about the origins of the former Frances Latimer. Lucius Dakers reported that Francis was a native of Laurens County. Levo Oliver (listed under "Sullivans") the granddaughter of Frances's sister, Emma, recalled that they grew up "somewhere in the country." We do know that Frances was literate, because there are family stories such as that told by Altamease Culver (another granddaughter of Frances's sister, Emma, discussed below under "Sullivans") who remembers her mother receiving 10-page letters from Frances with all the news of Laurens.

Bethel Hall Baptist Church in Hickory Tavern

Bethel Hall was established about 1910, on a 2.8 tract of land donated (and/or sold for a negligible amount) to the organizers by Wick and Frances Garrett. The church was originally named Charleston Hall Baptist Church before being renamed by Hattie Garrett, the oldest daughter of Wick and Frances. In addition to his role as an

the 1900 census (T1070, roll 45, Soundex) but this is probably an erroneous reference to "Otto" who was born in March of that year.

Wick saw to it that each of his children who desired to attend college did so: His oldest daughter, Hattie was a 1908 graduate of the Industrial Agricultural Memorial College of South Carolina, and was a school teacher; his son, John Wesley Garrett graduated from Allen University in 1926, which was also the alma mater of his foster son and grandnephew, Lucius Dakers. His oldest son, Fletcher Mills Garrett, graduated from South Carolina State; and daughter, Early (who became a nurse) and son, Thomas, also attended college.

Wick Garrett was a prosperous man who owned hundreds of acres of land, a circumstance that was quite unusual for a Black man of his time. Wick

THE SOURCE OF OUR PRIDE

Frances Garrett

Photograph identified as the young Frances

organizer, Wick Garrett served as one of the four original trustees of the church. The first pastor, the Rev. John H. Cunningham, served for five years; he ordained Wick Garrett (and Wick's son-in-law, Richard Neely, Jr.) among the church's first deacons.

The present structure of Bethel Hall was opened on May 20, 1973; Lucius Dakers was the keynote speaker. The Rev. Norman P. Pearson, the eighth pastor, was introduced to Bethel Hall by Wick's son, Shellie Donaldson Garrett. Dr. Pearson has served since 1964. Bethel Hall continues to play a role in the lives of the grandchildren, great-grandchildren, and other relatives of Wick and Frances Garrett. On January 2, 1994, the members of Bethel Hall dedicated a new Education Building; the program notes that Mrs. Tina Garrett (wife of Thomas Weldon Garrett, Sr.) served on the program committee, and

Marion Beasley (the grandson of Wick's sister, Early) and Dr. Robert Shortt (the husband of one of Early's great-granddaughters) served on the finance committee. Bethel Hall continues to play a role in the lives of the grandchildren and great-grandchildren of Wick and Frances Garrett. Many of Wick's grandchildren remain active members, including Mary Lee Garrett Thompson, Lnora Garrett Grayson, Frances Boston, Thomas Weldon Garrett, Sr., and until his death in 1998, Willie Carold Garrett. Over the last decade, Wick's female descendants have returned as guest speakers at the annual Bethel Hall Women's Day program, including great-granddaughter (then judge) Abigail Rogers Harris, granddaughter, Lila Lloyd, and great-granddaughter, LaBrenda Garrett-Nelson. On January 1, 1994, LaBrenda Garrett-Nelson was married at Bethel

Wick and his sons (circa 1918): first row: Cloda, Thomas, Wick, and Fletcher Mills; second row: Albert Elton, Shellie Donaldson, Otto, and John.

Hall in a ceremony performed by Pastor Pearson. Of course, a Sunday service at Bethel Hall is always a part of the program when the Garrett, Neely, and Sullivan families hold their biannual reunions in South Carolina.

The Charleston Hall Public Colored School

The Charleston Hall Public Colored School was established as one of the first public schools for African Americans in the area, when the organizers of Bethel Hall purchased 1.5 acres of land for one dollar from Wick and Frances Garrett, on July 7, 1913. Two of Wick's children, Fletcher Mills and Hattie, and two daughters-in-law, the former Alberta Barksdale (wife of Shellie Donaldson Garrett) and Mattie Neely Garrett, were teachers there. Many of Wick's grandchildren received their early educations at this school, including Shelly Ruth Rogers Kimpson, Celeste Harris,

Homer Neely, and all of the children of Albert Elton Garrett, I. In addition, many non-family members in the Hickory Tavern area attended the Charleston Hall Public Colored School. The ruins of the school can still be seen on Wilsontown Road, across from Bethel Hall.

Wick died on Dec. 2, 1928. His last will and testament is recorded in the Probate Court for Laurens County, filed in Estate File 783, Package 13, which document describes the Wick L. Garrett home place. The Dec. 6, 1928 edition of *the Laurens Advertiser* honored Wick by including an obituary entitled "Respected Colored Man Died Last Sunday."

Wick was the only African American mentioned on the page, which, coincidentally, also includes the obituary of a Confederate veteran of the Civil War. We can only wonder about how Wick Garrett managed to win respect outside the

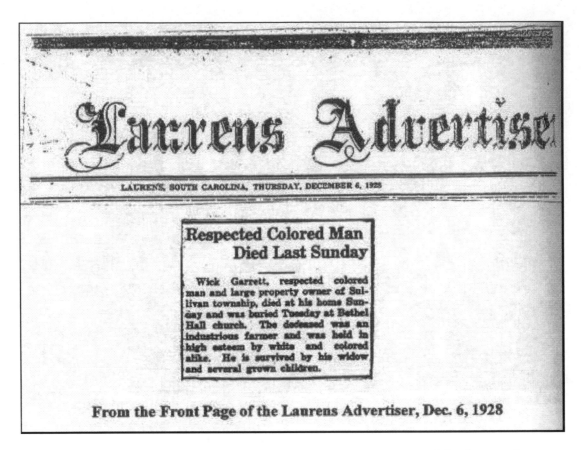

From the Front Page of the Laurens Advertiser, Dec. 6, 1928

Black community while maintaining his dignity and leaving his children a legacy of pride.

Wick's and C.G.'s Relationship

Although it is fairly certain that both Wick and C.G. were descended from Dublin, there is a question about their actual relationship. Ruth Simons Nicholson's immediate family referred to Wick Garrett as "Uncle Wick;" however, shortly before Ruth's death, she wrote a note to LaBrenda Garrett-Nelson, indicating that Wick and C.G. were first cousins, not siblings. A review of Ruth's files (now in the possession of her son, David Nicholson) failed to turn up any mention of Wick Garrett. Consistent with Ruth's correction; however, Wick's granddaughter, Mattie Elton Tucker remembers C.G. as "Cousin Cass."

C. G. was raised by his mother, so we should accept the accuracy of his published account (detailed above) that she had been brought from out-of-state, and so could not have been descended from Dublin. This means that C.G.'s father (identified by Nannie Allison as Hunter Garrett, contrary to the published report that his name was Samuel Garrett) must have been the link to Dublin.

Some of Wick's grandchildren say that Wick was fathered by a white man who was also the father of Wick's sister, Early. If Wick's father were white, his mother would have been Dublin's descendant. We know that Wick's mother married Ike Garrett after Wick and Early were born; however, it is possible that this relationship predated the "legal" marriage: Slaves could not enter into the legal state of marriage, and (unlike other Southern states) "South Carolina did not require former slaves to register their marriages and reveal how long they had lived together as man and wife.[28]" Thus, it is entirely possible that Wick's mother's husband was in fact his father (in which case, the light complexion of his skin, which probably gave rise to the story of a white father, would have been attributable to some earlier Caucasian ancestor; in this regard, note that we know from surviving photographs that both Ike Garrett and Wick's maternal grandmother were also obviously of mixed ancestry). Assuming that Ike Garrett was the link to Dublin, his mother would have been Dublin's daughter, and that would be consistent with C.G.'s identification of Dublin's daughter as his grandmother and Wick as his first cousin.

Early C. Beasley

Early Garrett (d. 1956) was the daughter of Ike and Hannah Garrett. She married Crockett Beasley (b. about 1840), and their children were Willie Jackson and Grace (Irby). The 1880 U.S. census lists Crockett and "Earline" Beasley, with four children: Mary, Lilla, Yancy, and an indecipherable name, all of whom are described as Black. The occupation listed for the first four names is farm laborer. Note that the birth date on Early's gravestone (1875) conflicts with the 1880 census record, the ages of her children, and reports by family members that Early and Wick were close in age.

Early's daughter, Grace Lee Irby played a leading role in establishing the Church of God in Laurens, and Early's great-great-grandson, Delpherd Barksdale, is now the pastor of the Evening Light Church of God in Laurens. Many of the children of Early's son, Willie Jackson Beasley, remained in Laurens, including C.D. Beasley, who founded the Beasley Funeral Home, and his brother Marion, now the proprietor of that establishment.

Dea. S.M. Garrett
Sam Garrett, From Flat Ruff's 120th Anniversary Program

Samuel M. Garrett

Samuel M. Garrett (b. Nov. 25, 1872, Laurens, S.C., d. Aug. 11, 1940) was identified as a first cousin by both C.G. and Wick Garrett, although his parents have yet to be identified. We do know that he married the former Hattie Hunter, and their children were Mamie (Kennedy), Carrie Lee (Williams), Alice Emma (Franklin), Jessie, and Florence. He was a deacon at Flat Ruff Baptist Church, and also served as the Sunday School Superintendent and the church secretary for many years.

Another Likely Relation: Stobo Garrett

The 1900 U.S. census lists a 47-year old Black male named Stobo Garrett (born in August 1852). No direct evidence of a familiar relationship has been discovered, however, several factors indicate that this

---

[28] *The Black Family in Slavery and Freedom* at p. 51.

person might be related to our Garretts. First there is the unusual name "Stobo"—the same name that one of Dublin's granddaughters gave to a son. There is also a Stobo Garrett of approximately the same age listed in Samuel Garrett's household in the 1870 U.S. census. The Stobo Garrett listed in the 1870 census named his sons Fletcher (born in April 1870), Hunter (born January 1886), Thomas (born October 1891), John (born August 1892), and Stobo Jr. (born November 1899)—all Garrett family names. The coincidence of these family names appearing in another family named "Garrett" warrants further investigation. Stobo's daughters were Janie (born May 1884), Sarah (born July 1887) and two indecipherable names (born in 1894 and 1897).

Lucius Dakers believes that this person may have been a relative he knew as "Stobo Mills," who ran an eating-place in the city of Laurens.

Other descendants of Samuel and Nancy Garrett are:

Carol Anderson, daughter of the former **Ruby Williams** and Charlie Walker **Latimer.**

Donald Jeffery Austin (b. Apr. 21, 1962) son of the former **Mable Lee Summers (see "Duncan")** and her first husband, Johnny Lee Austin.

Michael Anthony Austin (b. June 6, 1963) son of the former **Mable Lee Summers (see "Duncan")** and her first husband, Johnny Lee Austin.

Walter Darrell Austin (b. May 19, 1960) son of the former **Mable Lee Summers (see "Duncan")** and her first husband, Johnny Lee Austin.

Frederick Baker (b. May 26, 1968) son of **Bobby Fletcher Garrett**; he served in the U.S. Air Force, and has a daughter named Jasmine and a son named Rodney.

Jasmine Baker (b. June 1, 1989) the daughter of **Frederick Baker** and Veronica.

Frederick Baker

Rodney Baker (b. 199_) son of **Frederick Baker.**

The Rev. Delpherd ("Dale") Barksdale, son of the former **Kathryn** Beasley and Dial **Barksdale;** resident of Atlanta, Ga.; pastor of Evening Light Church of God in Laurens (where many Beasleys are members); married Jewel in 1996.

Kathryn Barksdale (b. Laurens, S.C.; TWIN to Kenneth) daughter of **Willie Jackson Beasley** and the former Katie Annette Wilson; married Dial Barksdale,[29] the father of her son, Dale, and daughter, Kendra; She graduated from Benedict college and is a teacher at Laurens District High School.

Kendra Barksdale, daughter of the former **Kathryn** Beasley and Dial **Barksdale.**

Ambria Marie Beasley, daughter of **Julius Augustus Beasley** and the former Shelia Robinson.

Bruce Beasley, son of **Jonathan Beasley** and Clara.

*****Cardell ("C.D.") Beasley** (b. July 1, 1917; d. Nov. 16, 1989, Laurens, S.C.) son of **Willie Jackson Beasley** and the former Katie Annette Wilson; founder of several businesses during his lifetime, including the Beasley funeral homes in Laurens and Fountain Inn, S.C., a barbershop, and a home for the aged. On Aug. 17, 1941, he married the former Lucinda Sherman (who retired as a school teacher in 1978, after many years assisting in the family businesses)[30] the mother of four children: Cardell, Jr., Carolyn (Shortt), Corneilia Elaine (Walker) and Cavernetta Sharon (Williams); he was also the father of Odell Beasley and Cora Altamease Lyons. C.D. served in the U.S. Navy during World War II," was elected to the Laurens County Council, and received the coveted Jefferson Award (presented by WYFF-TV) for meritorious service to a community in the Upstate. *The Laurens County Advertiser* devoted a full page to report on C.D.'s receipt of this award: C.D. helped register Black voters, offered aid to underprivileged youth, and operated an ambulance service for both Blacks and Whites (before there was an EMS system in Laurens County). As the late Hewlette Wasson[31] stated for the record,

"C.D. was really the man who furnished much of the leadership in promoting peaceful relations between the races [in Laurens County]."

Cardell Beasley, Jr., the son of **C.D. Beasley** and the former Lucinda Sherman; married the former Clara Briggs.

Cathy Beasley, daughter of **Garfield Beasley** and the former Clara Floyd.

Charles Debo Beasley, son of **Garfield Beasley** and the former Clara Floyd; attended the University of South Carolina; resides in Columbia, S.C..

Crystal Beasley, daughter of **Odell Beasley** and the former Mary Luster.

Garfield Beasley (b. May 16, 1932, Laurens, S.C.) the son of **Willie Jackson Beasley** and the former Katie Annette Wilson; he married the former Clara Floyd, fathering one son: Charles, and two daughters, Cathy and Clara (Moody); he is also the father of Elmira (Burton).

*****Hosea Beasley** (b., d. 1997, Laurens, S.C.) son of **Willie Jackson Beasley** and the former Katie Annette Wilson; he married the former Sarah Ann Cleveland, fathering four daughters.

Joanne Beasley, daughter of **Willie Edgar Beasley** and the former Evelyn Hill.

---

[29] Dial Barksdale was the foster son of Robert Nesbitt Neely (listed under Neelys) and his wife, the former Mildred Barksdale, and is also part of the same family as Alberta Barksdale, the wife of Shellie Donaldson Garrett. Thus, the children of Alberta and Shellie (Shelly Kimpson and Lila Lloyd) are related to Dial and Kathryn's children through both the Garretts and the Barksdales.

[30] Lucinda 's parents were Dr. Doyle Lee Sherman and Annie C. of Jacksonville, Florida; they were also the parents of three sons and three other daughters.

[31] The Wassons are White and they have been neighbors of the Black Garretts in Hickory Tavern for nearly a hundred years. Wick Garrett purchased land from Hewlette Wasson's grandmother (who was a Sullivan from the family after which Sullivan Township-which includes Hickory Tavern-was named). Hewlette Wasson (at the funeral of Albert Elton Garrett, I) spoke of the childhood illness that confined him to a wheelchair, noting that "Uncle Wick" was among the first visitors he had after being struck down. One of Hewlette Wasson's first acts upon becoming a probate judge was to assist Wick's widow in collecting a pension to which she was entitled; and among his last acts as a lawyer before his death in 1995, he handled the transfer of land once owned by Wick to two of Wick's great-grandchildren (Albert Elton Garrett, II and LaBrenda Garrett-Nelson) and assisted one of Wick's grandson in retiring on disability.

THE SECOND FRONT

The Laurens County Advertiser

A tribute long overdue

by Grant Vosburgh
Editor

For most people, a good wedding gets immediate reward. As Boy Scout gets his merit badge. The athlete gets his solution. The benefactor gets his one eminence — if not a healthy serve-off.

Every great now and then, however, the work of a good Samaritan goes unnoticed. Oh, one seems to him realize the sacrifices he makes and the lives he touches, but the public at large knows nothing about it.

But on that golden day when someone somewhere, finally puts a deserving spotlight on an individual, it arrives in special fashion, with short notice.

For C.D. Beasley, that day came on Thursday of last week, when he was one of five recipients of the coveted Jefferson Award, presented by WYFF-TV Greenville for meritorious service to a community in the state.

He swells with pride.

JEFFERSON AWARD — C.D. Beasley of Laurens proudly displays his glass-encased Jefferson Award medallion, given to him during a WYFF-TV banquet on Thursday. While the other four recipients were cited for single projects that benefitted their respective communities, Beasley's work spans two decades, and his unselfish deeds have touched many lives. (Photo by Grant Vosburgh)

"I would like to give thanks to all of the persons who worked with us. And when I say all the people, I mean black and white — everyone who enabled us to do these things."

— C.D. Beasley

C. D. Beasley

Some thoughts on a Jefferson Award winner ...

Wick's great-grandchildren (Albert Elton Garrett, II and

Jonathan Beasley, son of **Willie Jackson Beasley** and the former Katie Annette Wilson; married Clara, the mother of his sons, Marcus and Bruce; he is a retired school principal, residing in Beaufort, S.C..

Julius Augustus Beasley, son of Willie L. Beasley and the former Betty McDowell; married the former Sheila Robinson (a lawyer); one daughter: Ambria Marie; a minister; resides in Memphis, Tenn..

Kenneth Beasley (b. Laurens, S.C.; TWIN to Kathryn) son of **Willie Jackson Beasley** and the former Katie Annette Wilson.

Kenneth Edward Beasley (b. Oct. 23, 1964) son of **Marion Beasley** and the former Sarah Cunningham; graduated from Wofford College in 1987 and Gupton-Jones Mortuary College in 1991; now a mortician at Beasley Funeral Home, Inc; married the former Anedra Michelle Crosby,[32] on Nov. 25, 1995.

Marcus Beasley, son of **Jonathan Beasley** and Clara.

Marion Beasley (b. Aug. 8, 1933, Laurens, S.C.) son of **Willie Jackson Beasley** and the former Katie Annette Wilson; he married the former Sarah Cunningham[33] (a librarian at Fountain Inn Elementary School) the mother of his two children, Kenneth Edward and Simone Kay; he graduated from the Atlanta College of Mortuary Science in 1958 and is now the proprietor of Beasley Funeral Home, Inc., On Sept. 23, 1995, Marion was honored at a banquet at the Greenville-Spartanburg Marriott; his achievements are numerous, including that he is: the longest serving volunteer

Marion Beasley

member (more than 26 years) of the South Carolina Department of Probation, Parole, and Pardon Services, after being the first Black appointed in 1965; a 1985 recipient of the Order of the Palmetto by former governor Richard Riley of South Carolina; a former member of the Board of Directors of the United Way of Greenville County, the Greenville County Urban League, and the Chamber of Commerce Board of

---

[32] Anedra is the daughter of Drs. Willis and Margaree Crosby.

[33] At one time, west of the city of Laurens, the Cunninghams were one of only three Black families who were landowners; the other two were Garretts and Pooles (see Odessa Poole, listed below under Garretts). The Cunninghams include Bennie Cunningham who played pro football with the Pittsburgh Steelers in their glory days. According to the Spring 1998 edition of *The Foundation*, published by the African-American Historical Foundation of Laurens, South Carolina, the Cunninghams are descended from Priest Miller, identified in that publication as "the first Black landowner in Laurens County in the late 1800s'. Priest Miller married Sarah Clowney in 1878—note the possible relationship to the Dublin clan: one of Sally Mills's daughters married a Clowney. They had ten children: Ford, Mary, Judge, A.B., Ed, Suepearl, Rachel, Janie, Roxie, and Booker T. (the family's first college graduate). He and his family farmed 110 acres in the Mount Zion Community, and his grandchildren (the children of Roxie and Simon Cunningham) still reside on the family farm.

Fountain Inn. In addition to all of the Beasleys and the Mayor Pro Tempore of the City of Greenville, the banquet was attended by his Garrett cousins: Mr. and Mrs. Thomas Garrett, Sr. of Laurens, Mr. W. Paul Garrett of Brooklyn, N.Y., and Mrs. Lnora Grayson of Laurens.

Ladell Beasley, son of **Odell Beasley** and the former Mary Luster.

Odell Beasley, son of **C.D. Beasley;** married the former Mary Luster, the mother of his son, Ladell, and daughter, Crystal; owns several businesses in Charlotte, N.C., including, following in his father's footsteps, a funeral home.

Patricia Beasley, daughter of **Willie Edgar Beasley** and the former Evelyn Hill.

Robert ("Rob") Beasley, son of **Willie Edgar Beasley** and the former Evelyn Hill; married the former Annette Grant.

Simone Kay Beasley (b. Jan. 7, 1974) daughter of **Marion Beasley** and the former Sarah Cunningham; attends Hampton University.

Tony Beasley, son of **Willie Lee Beasley** and the former Betty McDowell, he has a son.

*Willie Edgar Beasley (b. Oct. 3, 1915, Laurens, S.C.; d. Dec. 27, 1985) son of **Willie Jackson Beasley** and the former Katie Annette Wilson; married the former Evelyn Hill, the mother of Evelyn (McDowell); Willie L.; Edna (Floyd); Robert; Joanne; and Patricia.

*Willie Jackson Beasley (b. Sept. 10, 1884, Laurens, S.C.; d. Oct 20, 1967) son of the former **Early Garrett** and Crockett **Beasley**. In 1914, he married the former Katie Annette Wilson (b. May 18, 1897) fathering 14 children: Willie Edgar, Cardell, Mildred (Young) Mamie Lee (Lynch) Ulysses, Jonathan, Hosea, Marjorie (Johnson) Crockett, Garfield, Marion, Katie Annette (Bland) and Twins: Kathryn (Barksdale) and Kenneth.[34]

Katie Annette Bland

Willie Lee ("Julius") Beasley, son of **Willie Edgar Beasley** and the former Evelyn Hill; he was drafted to play for the San Diego Chargers in 1965; married the former Betty McDowell (a graduate of Benedict College) the mother of his two sons, Julius Augustus and Tony.

*Lela Beeks (b. Laurens, S.C.; d.) daughter of **Ike and Hannah Garrett**.

Naajia Benjamin (b. Dec. 17, 1992) daughter of Tyrone Benjamin and **Nicole Price**.

Tyrone Benjamin, Jr. (b. Aug. 17, 1994) son of **Nicole Price**. and Tyrone Benjamin.

*(Katie) Annette Bland (b. Feb. 8, 1936, d. Aug. 17, 1997, Laurens, S.C.) daughter of **Willie Jackson**

---

[34] From the obituary of Katie Beasley.

Beasley and the former Katie Annette Wilson; she established her own successful business as the owner of Nat's Beauty in Laurens, S.C.; was married to Joseph Bland.

Cornell Bonaparte, son of **Julia Bonaparte.**

Julia Ann Bonaparte, daughter of **Talma Yeargins** and the former Corrie Brewster; she is the mother of Nicole Yeargins and Cornell Bonaparte.

Frances Boston (b. May 5, 1926, Laurens, S.C.) the fifth daughter of **Albert Elton Garrett, I and the former Mattie Neely**; she married Javan Boston;[35] and is the mother of six children: Betty Joann Garrett, Richard Charles Garrett, Marye Elaine (Hunter) Javan, Jr., Wister Paul, and John Nathan. Retired, she lives in Laurens, S.C.. Although her sister, Lnora Grayson is a close second, Frances is absolutely the best cook in the family, and her nieces and nephews have many fond memories of family gatherings at her home.

Jasnique Boston (b. May, 1983) daughter of (Wister) **Paul Boston** and the former Robin Allen.

Javan Boston, Jr. ("J Jr.") (b. Nov. 26, 1954, Laurens, S.C.) son of the former **Frances Garrett** and Javan **Boston**, Sr.; he has one daughter named Kayla Shaw.

John Nathan Boston ("Mickey") (b. Dec 2, 1959, Laurens, S.C.) son of the former **Frances Garrett** and Javan **Boston**, Sr.; he attended Johnson C. Smith College, in North Carolina; married Suzette; and has one daughter named Kourtney. A member of the U.S. Air Force, he served in Operation Desert Storm.

Kourtney Boston (b. November 1991) daughter of **John Nathan Boston** and Suzette.

Kayla Shaw, daughter of Javan Boston

(Wister) Paul Boston (b. Jan. 21, 1957, Laurens, S.C.) son of the former **Frances Garrett** and Javan **Boston**, he married the former Robin Allen[36] on Dec. 20, 1980, at New Grove Baptist Church in Laurens, S.C.; the couple have one daughter named Jasnique, and also raised Robin's cousin, Petrina Stevens. He graduated from South Carolina State College, and is a probation officer; he lives in Simpsonville, S.C..

Anthony Brown (b. Feb. 9, 1991) son of **Nicole Price.**

Derrell Brown (Mar. 31, 1989) son of **Nicole Price.**

---

[35] Javan was the youngest child of Max Boston and the former Mary Garrett (a member of the second African American family of Garretts, discussed above, d. March 1976); his siblings were: Marie (wife of Claude Massey); Sarah; Nathan (who married Sarah); Isaac (who married Daisy): and Max, Jr. The former Mary Garrett was the daughter of Caroline and Nathan Garrett

[36] Robin Allen is the daughter of the late Mrs. Maude Allen Sumpert.

Mr. & Mrs. John Nathan Boston

Paul Boston (in vest) with first cousins Bobbinetta Young, Jackie Garrett, Thomas Weldon Garrett, Jr., uncle Willie Carold Garrett, and Elp Garrett, II.

Anber N. Bumbrey, child of the former **Venessa Stoddard** and Derwin **Bumbrey.**

Julian A. Bumbrey, son of the former **Venessa Stoddard** and Derwin **Bumbrey.**

Venessa Bumbrey, daughter of the former **Ruth Williams** and Rosco **Stoddard;** married Derwin Bumbrey, the father of her children, Julian A. and Anber N.

Beryl Dakers Burton ("Mickey") daughter of **Lucius Dakers** and Lorraine; she is a television journalist at South Carolina public television station, ETV, following in the footsteps of her mother who was a newspaper reporter; she graduated from Syracuse University, and is the mother of a son, Jarrett, and a daughter, Brittney; resides in Columbia, S.C..

Brittney Burton, daughter of **Beryl Dakers Burton.**

Corey Burton, son of the former **Penny Smith** and John Edward **Burton.**

Elmira ("Penny") Burton, daughter of **Garfield Beasley** and the former Mamie Smith (the first wife of Bobby Fletcher Garrett)[37]; she married John Edward Burton, and is the mother of two children: Johndelin (a daughter) and Corey (a son).

Jarrett Burton, son of **Beryl Dakers Burton.**

---

[37] Thus, Penny Burton is the half-sister of Bobbinetta Young, listed below under "Garretts."

Frances Boston surrounded by six of her grandchildren and her twin great-granddaughters (1999)

Third Cousins: Beryl Dakers Burton and Bessie Crosson (listed under Neelys) (1983)

Johndeline Burton, daughter of the former **Penny Smith** and John Edward **Burton.**

Ruth Eider Butcher (b. Apr. 16, 1904) daughter of **Casper George Garrett** and the former Anna M. Threewitts; she married Ira Valentine and then William B. Butcher.

Cynthia W. Caldwell, daughter of **Daisy Griffin,** she is a resident of Greenville, S.C..

***Beulah Cora Cleveland** (b. May 9, 1887, Laurens S.C.) daughter of **Wick Lee Garrett** and the former Francis Latimer; married first to (and was widowed by) **Richard Neely, Jr.** (see his entry for the names of their children).

***Edward Coker** (d.) son of **Shellie Donaldson Garrett** and Elizabeth Coker (the sister of Thomas Garrett's wife, Lillian); never married; no children.[38]

***Celeste Coleman** (b. Laurens, S.C.) daughter of **Wick Lee Garrett** and the former Frances Latimer; she married Ernest Coleman, and was the mother of one son, Alfred Lavon.

***Dimitris Coleman,** son of **Alfred Lavon Coleman** and Sarah.

Alfred Lavon Coleman (b. Oct. 24, 1929) son of the former **Celeste Garrett** and Ernest **Coleman,** he married Sarah; had one son named Dimitris and stepchildren.

---

[38] SOURCE: Thomas W. Garrett, Sr.

Beulah Garrett Neely Cleveland

Creselene Dakers

Camara Dakers (b. Feb. 22, 1982) daughter of **Edwin Dakers** and the former Gail Bell.

Caroline Dakers (b. Mar. 30, 1952) daughter of **Creselene Dakers.**

Creselene Dakers (b. Aug. 26, 1921) daughter of **Pearl Irby Dakers** and foster child of Wick Lee Garrett; she is the mother of two sons: John and Edwin, and one daughter, Caroline.

Edwin Dakers (b. Dec.4, 1954) son of **Creselene Dakers**; he married the former Gail Bell and fathered two children: Jason and Camara.

Jason Dakers (b. Apr. 26, 1979) son of **Edwin Dakers** and the former Gail Bell.

Jerome Dakers, son of **Pearl Irby Dakers**; resides in Augusta, Ga.; has a daughter named Ruby.

John Dakers ("Buster") (b. Jan. 9, 1939) son of **Creselene Dakers** and Alfred Coleman,[39] he married

---

[39] Alfred Coleman's parents, John Frank and Elizabeth Coleman, are buried at Bethel Hall. John Frank's mother—Sal Coleman—was a Shell before marriage; Also, John Frank Coleman was the brother of Ernest Coleman; Ernest Coleman was the father of Alfred Lavon Coleman (listed above under Garretts). Thus, Alfred Lavon Coleman is a first cousin, once removed, to John Dakers (in addition to being a second cousin, once removed, on his mother's side). See also the listing for Lillian Maude Townsend (under Neelys, below) whose mother was a Coleman.

*John Dakers (in glasses) with (from right)
Thomas Weldon Garrett, Jr., Elp Garrett, II,
Kevin Garrett, Todd Dakers (his son),
and Willie Harold Garrett (1998)*

Lucius Dakers and Elp Garrett, II (1998)

the former Harriet Jernigan, the mother of his three children: Todd, Karen, and Kenneth; he attended Baylor University and Florida State while serving a 30-year tour in the U.S. Army, including 14 years as a medic in the Green Berets; resides in Laurens, S.C..

Karen Michelle Dakers (b. Dec. 6, 1967) daughter of **John Dakers** and the former Harriet Jernigan; attending Staten Island University.

Kenneth Michael Dakers (b. June 11, 1970) son of **John Dakers** and the former Harriet Jernigan; attending Greenville Tech., Art, Design.

Lucius Warren Dakers (b. 1915) the son of **Pearl Irby Dakers** and foster child of Wick Lee Garrett; he

married Lorraine (a newspaper reporter) the mother of his daughter, Beryl (Burton); he graduated from—and was the longtime president of the alumni association of—Allen University; resides in Columbia, S.C..

Pearl Irby Dakers, daughter of the former **Dicey Garrett** and Lee **Irby**; the mother of Lucius, Creselene, Jerome, and James Marion Irby.

Todd Keith Dakers (b. May 12, 1963) son of **John Dakers** and the former Harriet Jernigan; attended Piedmont Tech.

Ruby Dakers, daughter of **Jerome Dakers**; last known residence was in New Jersey.

*****Syble Davis,** daughter of **Albert Elton Garrett**, I.

Shirona Denny, daughter of the former **Wanda Grayson** and her second husband, Barry **Denny**.

Marian Davis Dixon (d. Oct. 26, 1967) daughter of **Christopher Threewitts Garrett** and the former Charlesena Davis.

Mable Lee Summers Austin Duncan (b. Aug. 5, 1941) daughter of the former **Alma** Yeargins and Henry **Summers**; married first to Johnny Lee Austin, the father of her three sons: Walter, Donald, and Michael; second marriage to Albert Duncan.

Christopher Durham (b. July 27, 1984) son of **Evangeline Price**.

Alice Franklin, daughter of **Samuel Garrett** and the former Hattie Hunter; married Pluma Franklin, the father of her son, Otis.[40]

Otis Franklin, son of the former **Alice Garrett** and Pluma **Franklin**.

Jennifer Ferguson (b. 1964) daughter of the former **Phyllis Threewitts Simons** and Dr. Richard **Ferguson**; dancer and actress.

Jocelyn Ferguson (b. 1959) daughter of the former **Phyllis Threewitts Simons** and Dr. Richard **Ferguson**; obtained associate degree from Seattle Central College; bachelor degree from University of Washington; Masters degree from University of California, at Berkely; doctorate in art history at Berkeley.

Kay Madeline Ferguson (b. 1955) daughter of the former **Phyllis Threewitts Simons** and Dr. Richard Ferguson; graduated from Washington State University; graduate work in Spanish and Portuguese at Howard and Georgetown Universities.

Norman Richard Ferguson (b. July 15, 1953) son of the former **Phyllis Threewitts Simons** and Dr. Richard **Ferguson**; married and divorced Monica Leonard.

Denise Fredericks

Phyllis Threewitts Ferguson (b. Aug. 20, 1926) daughter of the former **Mattie Phyllis Garrett** and Alfred **Simons**; married Dr. Richard Ferguson (a colonel in the U.S. Air Force and a dentist) the father of her four children: Norman Richard; Kay Madeline; Jocelyn; and Jennifer; graduated from Howard University.

Edna Floyd, daughter of **Willie Edgar Beasley** and the former Evelyn Hill; married.

Denise Fredericks (b. June 15, 1956) daughter of **Thomas Weldon Garrett, Sr.** and the former Eva Mae Smith; twice married: first to the late Edward Herbert Mack, the father of her only child: Edward Herbert Mack, Jr., then to Eugene Fredericks (a native of the

---

40 SOURCE: Lillie Williams-Tims, African American Historical Society of Laurens, South Carolina.

Denise and Eugene Fredericks

Jumoke Gamble with his parents (1998)

U.S. Virgin Islands)[41]; attended Bronx Community and City College, City University of New York. On June 22, 1994, she received a Labor Relations Management Award in recognition of her efforts in establishing one of the first Labor-Management Partnership Councils, at the Federal Emergency Management Director's Award Ceremony that was held in Washington, D.C.; resides in Laurens on land once owned by her great-grandfather, Wick Garrett.

Afiya Layla Gamble (b. Aug. 8, 1977) daughter of the former **Madeline Tucker** and Raymond **Gamble** Jr.

Jumoke Gamble (b. Aug. 9, 1974) son of the former **Madeline Tucker** and Raymond **Gamble**, Jr.

Madeline Gamble ("Leany") (b. May 31, 1949; Twin to Evangeline) daughter of the former **Mattie Elton Garrett** and Edward Jordan **Tucker**, Sr.; married Raymond Gamble, Jr. the father of her two children: Jumoke and Afiya; graduated from Queens College, City University of New York; received her doctorate in 1996.

*****Albert Elton Garrett** ("Elp") (b. July 31, 1895, Laurens, S.C.; d. Nov. 23, 1985) the son of **Wick Lee Garrett** and the former Frances Latimer. He was a farmer and blacksmith, served as a private in the U.S. Army, and was a devoted member of Bethel Hall Baptist Church where he was the Sunday School Superintendent, after becoming the church's

---

[41] Eugene Fredericks is a first cousin to members of the popular singing group "Full Force."

The Young Albert Elton Garrett, I

Seated: John and Missie Neely, Mattie Neely Garrett, Elp, and grandchildren, Richard and Joann Garrett. Standing: Frances, Mary, Jeruther, Nora, Ruby Pearl, and twins, Harold and Carold

youngest deacon at the age of 22. Elp did not desire to follow in the footsteps of his siblings who went off to college, so Wick insisted that Elp learn a trade; that is how Elp ended up as a blacksmith. Elp married the former **Mattie Neely** on Dec. 28, 1919, the mother of eleven of his children: Mattie Elton (Tucker); Jeruther; Twins: Wister Pickney (Paul) and Mary Lee (Thompson); Ruby Pearl; Frances Patricia (Boston); Missie Lnora (Grayson); Thomas Weldon; Bobby Fletcher; and Twins: Willie Harold and Willie Carold. He was also the father of Syble Garrett Davis (deceased), Talma Yeargins, and Mrs.

Alma Summers. On Dec. 26, 1976, Elp and Mattie were honored at a banquet, hosted by their children to celebrate their 57th wedding anniversary. Although he had little formal education, he knew the Bible by heart.[42]

---

[42] SOURCE: **Harold Carter**, who grew up in Hickory Tavern; his grandmother, who was a Hood, was known to GNS family members as "Cousin Tack." Harold Carter is also related to John Dakers (listed above under Garretts), because Harold Carter's grandfather—Allen Shell—and John Daker's great-grandmother—Sal Shell Coleman—were brother and sister.

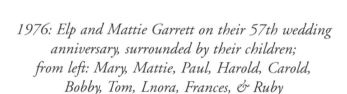

1976: Elp and Mattie Garrett on their 57th wedding anniversary, surrounded by their children; from left: Mary, Mattie, Paul, Harold, Carold, Bobby, Tom, Lnora, Frances, & Ruby

Albert Elton Garrett, II and his family

Albert Elton Garrett, II (b. July 14, 1958, in Laurens, S.C.) son of **Thomas Weldon Garrett, Sr.** and the former Eva Mae Smith; married the former Denise Worrell (a graduate of Bernard Baruch College, City University of New York, and now a U.S. Postal service executive) fathering two sons: Albert Elton Garrett, III and Thomas Alexander; resides in Hickory Tavern, S.C., on land that was once owned by his great-grandfather, Wick Garrett.

The Maternal Grandparents of Elp Garrett, II's
children: Alexander Worrell, Sr. and the former
Pearl Hendricks, with son

Albert Elton Garrett, III (b. Jan. 25, 1980) son of
Albert Elton Garrett, II and the former Denise
Worrell. Albert is a star athlete but his family is most
proud of his academic achievements. He attends
Newberry College, in Newberry, S.C.

Bobby & Alice Garrett

Bobby Garrett, surrounded by three of his daughters and grandchildren

A.C. Garrett, son of Emma and **Wade Garrett**; the father of Anne (Jeffcoat).

Arlen Garrett, son of **Christopher Threewitts Garrett, III** and Portia.

Bobby Fletcher Garrett (b. May 3, 1934, Laurens, S.C.) son of **Albert Elton Garrett, I and the former Mattie Neely**; married Mamie Smith (of Laurens County) and then, on June 16, 1979, the former Alice Jane McCullough (assistant principal; graduated from Allen University; masters from Fordham University; doctorate in education from University of North Carolina, Chapel Hill);[43] retired Postal worker; five children: Bobbinetta (Young); Barbara Rochelle (b. Nov. 25, 1966; the mother of four);

Nicole (b. Apr. 19, 1975); Frederick Baker; and Chaunte; stepson: Jay; resides in Raleigh, N.C.

*Casper George Garrett, Jr. (b. Mar. 1, 1895) son of **Casper George Garrett** and the former Anna M. Threewitts; married the former Cornice Gertrude Christie on Dec. 13, 1917; as remembered by Josephine Simons Wade, he co-authored a play with Langston Hughes, although we found no evidence the play was ever produced.

Chaunte Garrett (b. Feb. 16, 1981) daughter of **Bobby Fletcher Garrett** and the former Alice Jane McCullough; youngest grandchild of Albert Elton and Mattie Garrett. She attends North Carolina A&T.

---

[43] the daughter of Malachi McCullough.

Chanute Garrett

*Chester Garrett, son of **Wade Garrett**; father (by his second marriage to Mag) of Willie James, Leroy, Wade, Eunice (Ramage) and Emma; he was also the father by a previous marriage of twin boys (Ludie and Arthur) both of whom died in a house fire as children.

Christopher Threewitts Garrett (b. Feb. 25, 1909; d. Jan. 15, 1967) son of **Casper George Garrett** and the former Anna M. Threewitts; married the former Charlesena Davis on Aug. 25, 1926, the mother of Christopher Threewitts, Jr. and Marian (Dixon); second marriage to the former Rachelle Robinson on Jan. 27, 1950, the mother of sons Ralston and Franklin.

Christopher Threewitts Garrett, Jr. (b. Oct. 26, 1926) son of **Christopher Threewitts Garrett** and the former Charlesena Davis; attended Allen University; resides in Washington, D.C.; one son: Christopher Threewitts Garrett, III.

Christopher Threewitts Garrett, III, son of **Christopher, Threewitts Garrett, Jr.**; obtained masters degree in architecture from Catholic University in D.C.; married Portia, the mother of his son, Arlen; resides in Washington, DC.

*Cloda Garrett (b. Sept. 22, 1892; d. August 3, 1920) a son of **Wick Garrett** and the former Francis J. Latimer; he served in France, during WW I.

*Colon Hunter Garrett, Sr. son of **Casper George Garrett** and the former Anna M. Threewitts; graduated from Meharry Dental School in 1927 after obtaining degree from Lincoln University; the father of three sons: Colon, Jr., George, and Reverdy.

*Colon Hunter Garrett, Jr. (b. Nov. 1, 1919; d. Feb. 1996) son of **Colon Hunter Garrett, Sr.**; resided in Philadelphia, PA.

Craig Garrett (b. Apr. 21, 1967) son of **(Betty) Joanne Garrett**.

Danielle Garrett (b. Apr. 8, 1982) daughter of **Thomas Weldon Garrett, Jr.** And the former Leslie Hall.[44] She plans to enter St. John's University in the fall of 2000.

Debra Jean Garrett (b. Laurens, S.C.) daughter of **Ruby Pearl Garrett** and Hammer Algood; mother of Rosalynd, Michael Antonio ("Tony") and Terrence.

Dominique Garrett (b. May 7, 1983) daughter of **Tyrone Garrett**.

(Caspar) George Garrett (b. Oct. 19, 1929) son of Dr. **Colon Hunter Garrett, Sr.**.

---

[44] Leslie Hall is the daughter of Kenmore E. Hall (whose parents were from Barbados) and the former Georgianna Maynard (whose parents hailed from Nevis).

Danielle Garrett

Fletcher Mills Garrett

Emma Garrett, daughter of **Chester Garrett** and Mag.

*****Fletcher Mills Garrett** (b. Apr 9, 1885, Laurens, S.C.; d. Mar. 13, 1964) the eldest son of **Wick Lee Garrett** and the former Frances Latimer, married Mary Finley Washington (b. Feb. 2, 1887; d. Oct. 15, 1953); one daughter (Lois Williams) and one stepdaughter (Bernice Garlington) graduated from South Carolina State College, in Orangeburg, S.C., and taught in the Laurens County schools for more than 28 years.

Florence Garrett (b. Oct. 1893, Laurens, S.C.) daughter of **Sam Garrett** and the former Hattie Hunter.

Franklin Garrett, son of **Christopher Threewitts Garrett** and the former Rachelle Robinson.

*****Hattie Garrett** (b. Mar. 12, 1884, Laurens, S.C.; d. Dec. 26, 1913) the eldest daughter of **Wick Lee Garrett** and the former Frances Latimer; graduated from Industrial Agricultural Memorial College of South Carolina in 1908. Tragically, Hattie contracted tuberculoses while away at college; she died after teaching for only about a year. Mary Garrett Thompson has her college degree.

Jeruther Garrett, a beloved aunt

Jackie Garrett with son and grandson (1999)

Jacqueline Garrett (b. Aug. 25, 1949, Laurens, S.C.) daughter of **Thomas Weldon Garrett, Sr.** and the former Eva Mae Smith; married and divorced Steve Murray; one son: Demaunt Shannon Robinson (son of Don Robinson, a graduate of Lincoln University). A longtime underwriter with the New York Life Insurance Company, she relocated with that company from New York City To Atlanta, Ga., in 1995.

Jamilia Garrett (b. Apr. 1, 1982) daughter of **Tyrone Garrett**.

*Jeruther ("Ruth") Garrett** (b. Apr. 15, 1922, Laurens, S.C.; d. June 12, 1962), daughter of **Albert Elton Garrett, I and the former Mattie Neely**. She died an untimely death at the age of 40.

Jessie Garrett (b. July 27, 1899, Laurens, S.C.) child of **Sam Garrett** and the former Hattie Hunter.

(Betty) Joann Garrett (b. Aug. 22, 1944, Laurens, S.C.) daughter of the former **Frances Garrett (see "Boston")**; mother of Teresa and Craig; resides in Washington, D.C.

John Wesley Garrett

Joann Garrett (far right) with her mother, daughter, and twin granddaughters

*John B. Garrett, a cousin remembered by Josephine Wade; he was a doctor at Tuskegee; he had a son who was a dentist; died in Boston, Mass.

*John Wesley Garrett (b. Jan. 9, 1902, Laurens S.C.; d. August 1983) a son of **Wick Lee Garrett** and the former Frances Latimer; graduated from Allen University in 1926; taught in the public schools of Laurens and Newberry Counties for about 20 years; married the former Sweetie Bell Peterson. At the time of his death he was employed by his cousins, at the Beasley Funeral Home.

Kevin Garrett, son **of Paul Garrett** and the former Leanease White.

Kevin Garrett (far right) with father, brother, sister, and Jackie Garrett

Brothers: Kevin and Tyrone Garrett

First Cousins Lathia & Tony Garrett, with Great-grandfather, Elp Garrett, I

Kimberly Garrett (b. May 5, 1967) daughter of **Paul Garrett** and the former Leanease White.

Lathia Garrett (b. 1980, Laurens, S.C.) daughter of **Thomas Wayne Garrett** and Myrt McDow; the mother of a son.

*****Leroy Garrett,** son of **Chester Garrett** and Mag.

*****Maceo Fleming Garrett**, son of **Casper George Garrett** and the former Anna M. Threewitts; served in WW I.

Marcus Garrett (b. Mar. 2, 1983) son of **Richard Charles Garrett** and the former Barbara Graden.

*****Marion Threewitts Garrett,** son of **Casper George Garrett** and the former Anna M. Threewitts; attended South Carolina State.

Dr. Naomi Mills Garrett, Ph. D. (b. Aug. 24, 1906) daughter of **Casper George Garrett** and the former Anna M. Threewitts; graduate of Benedict College; obtained masters degree from Atlanta University; she was the first Black to complete the degree requirements for a Ph.D. in Romance Languages at Columbia University (the second African American to obtain this degree there); after retiring as a professor of French and Spanish from the West Virginia State College and Institute, she was appointed a university professor at Denison University, Granville, Ohio; she also lectured in French for the U.S. government in Senegal; a former Fulbright, Ford, and Rosenwald fellow, she is included in "Who's Who of American Women" and "Biography of American Scholars."

*****Otto Garrett** (b. Mar. 11, 1900, Laurens, S.C.; d. Sept. 6, 1919) son of **Wick Lee Garrett** and the former Frances Latimer; in a case of mistaken identity, Otto was shot by a white man as he was coming out

DR. NAOMI GARRETT

Dr. Garrett Takes Post At Denison

Dr. Naomi Garrett, retiring professor of modern foreign languages at West Virginia State College, has been appointed a university professor at Denison University, Granville, Ohio.

Dr. Garrett, who will complete 25 years at WVSC this spring, was a visiting lecturer at Denison last semester. Her new post was created in 1970 and entails teaching courses related to several academic areas. She will emphasize African literature of French and English expression, and the literature of the West Indies and French Caribbean.

Dr. Garrett participated in a conference on Negritude in Dakar, Senegal, last year at the invitation of the Senegal president. A former Fulbright, Ford and Rosenwald fellow, she is included in "Who's Who of American Women," "Dictionary of International Biography," and "Biography of American Scholars."

A world traveler, Dr. Garrett has visited Europe, the Middle East Asia, the Orient, North Africa, the West Indies and parts of Latin America. At West Virginia State she has served many years as advisor for foreign students.

W. Paul Garrett

of Mount Anthony church; the white man claimed that Otto had a gun, and nothing was ever done.

*Paul (born Wister Pickney) Garrett** (b. June 17, 1923, d. April 29, 1998; (Twin to Mary Lee) Laurens, S.C.) is the eldest son of **Albert Elton Garrett, I and the former Mattie Neely**; now retired, he served in U.S. Army during WW II: married the former Leanease White, and had three children: Tyrone, Kevin, and Kimberly; his first marriage was to the former Addie Brown.

Rachelle Garrett (b. Nov. 20, 1985) daughter of **(Willie) Harold Garrett, Jr.** and the former Sheniqua Kiantha Devalle Young.

Ralston Garrett, son of **Christopher Threewitts Garrett** and the former Rachelle Robinson.

*Ralston Proudfit Garrett** (b. Feb. 5, 1893; d. May 15, 1960)) son of **Casper George Garrett** and the former Anna M. Threewitts; named after the white man with whom his father read law; served in the U.S. Army during WW I; the biological father of Frances (who was adopted by Ralston's parents).

Reverdy ("Buck") Ransom Garrett (b. Apr. 21, 1931) son of **Colon Hunter Garrett, Sr.**; resident of Philadelphia, Pa..

Richard Charles Garrett ("Dicky") (b. Oct 28, 1946) son of the former **Frances Garrett (see "Boston")**; married and divorced the former Barbara Graden (who attended Johnson C. Smith College in North Carolina) the mother of his son, Marcus; graduated from Vorhees College in South Carolina, and obtained a Masters degree from Clemson University; served in the U.S. Army during the Vietnam War; lives in Greenville, S.C..

*Richard Garrett, his son (Marcus)
and uncle (Bobby Garrett)*

*Shellie Donaldson Garrett, his wife (Alberta) and
daughters (Lila and Shelly Ruth)*

Rosalynd Garrett (b. June 16, 1983, Laurens, S.C.) daughter of Glenn Bishop and **Debra Jean Garrett**.

Ruby Pearl Garrett (b. July 16, 1925, Laurens, S.C.) daughter of **Albert Elton Garrett, I and the former Mattie Neely**; two children: Thomas Wayne and Debra Jean.

*****Shellie Donaldson Garrett** (b. June 20, 1898, Laurens, S.C.; d. Nov. 7, 1965) son of **Wick Lee Garrett** and the former Frances Latimer; married Alberta Barksdale (d. August 1983) fathering three children: Shelly Ruth (Rogers Kimpson) and Twins: Lila (Lloyd) and Lillian (the latter died in infancy); also the father of Vivian Sullivan and Edward Coker (deceased). For many years he made his home in the Bethel Hall Community where he farmed land he inherited from his father, Wick Garrett. Shellie and

his wife met the Rev. Norman Pearson and his wife when they moved to Greenville, took the young couple under their wings, and introduced them to Bethel Hall.

Tahitia ("Tommi") Garrett (b. Oct. 15, 1977) daughter of **Tyrone Garrett**.

Teresa Garrett (b. Sept. 2, 1965, raised in Laurens, S.C.) daughter of **(Betty) Joanne Garrett**; mother of Twins: Brittni and Bridjet Russell; resides in Brooklyn, N.Y..

Terrence Garrett (b. Dec. 29, 1986, Laurens, S.C.) son of Jimmy Redd and **Debra Jean Garrett**.

*****Thomas Garrett** (b. December 1889, Laurens, S.C.) son of **Wick Lee Garrett** and the former Frances Latimer; married the former Lillian Coker;

Chaunte, Terence, Danielle, and Rosalynd Garrett

Thomas Wayne Garrett

they maintained homes in Laurens, S.C. and Tampa, Florida; he was a college graduate who made his living as an insurance salesman.

Thomas Alexander Garrett (b. Aug. 21, 1985) son of **Albert Elton Garrett, II** and the former Denise Worrell.

(Thomas) Wayne Garrett (b. 1954, Laurens, S.C.) son of **Ruby Pearl Garrett** and Hammer Algood; married the former Judy Adams, the mother of his daughter, Whitney; and his son, Thomas, Jr.; also the father of Lathia; served in the U.S. Army; resides in Greenville, S.C..

Thomas Wayne Garrett, Jr. (b. March 1996) son of **Thomas Wayne Garrett** and the former Judy Adams.

Mrs. Thomas Wayne Garrett (Judy) and daughter, Whitney

Thomas Weldon Garrett, Jr. and family

Thomas Weldon Garrett, Jr. (b. June 3, 1957) son of **Thomas Weldon Garrett, Sr.** and the former Eva Mae Smith; graduated from Hunter College, City University of New York and received an MA from the State University of New York (Empire State); sales executive; married the former Leslie Hall (a graduate of Medgar Evers College, City University of New York, obtained masters degree from Brooklyn Polytech) the mother of his only child: Danielle; resides in Staten Island, N.Y.

The children of Thomas Weldon Garrett, Sr.:
Tom, Jr., Jackie, Denise, LaBrenda, and Elp

Thomas Weldon Garrett, Sr. (b. Mar. 1, 1933, Laurens, S.C.) son of **Albert Elton Garrett, I and the former Mattie Neely;** his first marriage was to the former Eva Mae Smith, a daughter of Susie Bell and Arnex Smith;[45] the children of this marriage are: Jacqueline (formerly, Murray); LaBrenda (Garrett-Nelson, formerly Stodghill and Bowman); Denise (Fredericks, formerly Mack); Thomas, Jr.; and Albert Elton, II; his second marriage was to Estella Valdespee; his third and last marriage was to the former Ernestine (Tina) Straus. He is a Deacon at Bethel Hall Baptist Church in Hickory Tavern; retired from Phelps Dodge Refining Company after 27 years, now the owner of Garrett Asphalt & Gravel in Laurens County, in partnership with his daughter Denise, residing on Garrett Drive in Hickory Tavern, on land once owned by his paternal grandfather, Wick Garrett. He served in the U.S. Army during the Korean War; two stepchildren: Jacqueline McKinnon (the mother of three: Nya Creary; Kumba Creary, and Imani McKinnon) and Gary Straus (father of a daughter, also named Imani).

---

[45] The former Susie Bell Vance (b. 1913; d. 1978) was the only child of Allen Vance and the former Josie Burton (who, we are told, was of Native American descent); Arnex Smith was the son of Thomas Smith and the former Martha Jackson; Martha Jackson was the daughter of Curtis Jackson. The former Susie Bell Vance and Arnex Smith were also the parents of Thomas, Ethel, Arnex, Jr. (deceased) and David Lee.

Garrett Gravel & Asphalt: Tom, Sr., in cab of
truck, and son , Elp, II

The maternal ancestors of Tom Garrett's Children:

Susie Bell Smith

Mrs. Thomas Weldon Garrett, Sr. (Tina)

Allen Vance (right) and his brother

Josie Burton Vance

First Cousins Lathia & Tony Garrett, with Great-grandfather, Elp Garrett, I

Tony (Michael Antonio) Garrett (b. Oct. 10, 1981, Laurens, S.C.) son of Yancy Williams and **Debra Jean Garrett**.

Tyrone Garrett (b. Aug. 13, 1958) son of **Paul Garrett** and the former Leanease White; married; three daughters: Tahitia; Jamilia, and Dominique.

Tyrone Garrett and Elp Garrett, II

* **Wade Garrett** Wister Lee Garrett identified as a first cousin; first wife was mother of son, Chester; second wife, Emma, was mother of A.C.

Thomas Garrett (top center), his wife (the former Lillian Coker), and members of her family

Albert Elton Garrett, III, with grandparents (Thomas Weldon Garrett, Sr. and Eva M. Garrett)

Frances and Javan Boston, Sr. surrounded by children (Mickey, Richard, Paul and Joann), grandchildren (Teresa and Marcus) brothers (Carold, Harold, and Tom), and daughters-in-law (Suzette, Robin, and Barbara) and family friend (Dot)

*Wade Garrett, son of Mag and **Chester Garrett.**

Whitney Garrett, daughter of **Thomas Wayne Garrett** and the former Judy Adams.

*(Willie) Carold Garrett ("Cack") (b. Mar. 5, 1936, d. March 6, 1998; Twin to Willie Harold, Laurens, S.C.) son of **Albert Elton Garrett, I and the former Mattie Neely;** married the former Ruby Nell Johnson, one son: Michael Suber; deacon, Bethel Hall Baptist Church in Hickory Tavern; lived in Laurens, S.C.

Harold and Carold

Thomas Weldon Garrett, Sr., Willie Carold Garrett, and the Rev. Norman P. Pearson

(Willie) Harold Garrett ("Hack") (b. Mar. 5, 1936; TWIN to Willie Carold Laurens, S.C.) son of **Albert Elton Garrett, I and the former Mattie Neely Garrett**; married and divorced Priscilla Higgins; two children: Harold, Jr., and Phyllis (Latimer); second marriage to the former Mamie Anderson; lives in Hodges, S.C.

(Willie) Harold Garrett, Jr. (b. Laurens, S.C.) son of (Willie) Harold Garrett and the former Priscilla Higgins; married the former Sheniqua Kiantha DeValle Young, the mother of his daughter, Rachelle.

Willie James Garrett, a son of Mag and **Chester Garrett**; resident of Greenwood, S.C.

Harold Garrett, Jr. and Mike Suber

Mrs. Willie Carold Garrett (Ruby Nell)

Mr. and Mrs. Harold Garrett, Sr. (Mamie)

From the front page of USA TODAY, June 24, 1986

LaBrenda Garrett-Nelson (b. Apr. 21, 1953, Laurens, S.C.) daughter of **Thomas Weldon Garrett, Sr.** and the former Eva Mae Smith; one child: Alexis Garrett (Bowman) Stodghill; tax lawyer, admitted to the bar of New York, Washington, D.C., and South Carolina; served on the staff of the U.S. Congress Joint Committee on Taxation (1982-87, during her tenure there her photograph was featured in the June 24, 1986, cover story of USA TODAY, in both the domestic and international editions); was an adjunct professor in the graduate division of the Georgetown University Law Center from 1987-91; currently a partner in the in the big five accounting firm of Ernst & Young. She graduated from John Jay College of Criminal Justice (B.A., 1975), City University of New York, and obtained both a Law Degree (Juris Doctor, 1978) and a Masters of Law (in taxation, 1982) from New York University School of Law. She was married three times: first to Reginald Harding Bowman (biological father of Alexis; attended John Jay College of Criminal Justice) then to Charles Derrick Stodghill (lawyer, Morehouse College and New York University School of Law; U.S. Justice Department; adoptive father of Alexis) and on Jan. 1, 1994, at Bethel Hall Baptist Church in Hickory Tavern, to Paul Neal Nelson. [46] She and her husband

---

[46] Paul Neal Nelson is a son of Rainey Nelson, Sr. and the former Lily Young of Georgetown, SC..; has served as assistant pastor at New Macedonia Baptist Church and associate minister at Union Temple Baptist church, in Washington, D.C.; He retired from the staff of the U.S. Congress House Budget Committee after 28 years of service, and is the father, by a previous marriage, of Charrisse Dianne, Charlene, and (Paul) Neal, Jr.

LaBrenda & daughter, Alexis (1988)

LaBrenda and Paul, and their daughters,
Charrisse and Alexis (1994)

maintain homes in Washington, D.C. and in
Hickory Tavern, S.C. on land once owned by her
great-grandfather, Wick Garrett. She is a Life member of the African American Historical Foundation
of Laurens, South Carolina. She began to compile
the information contained in this biographical history in 1979.

LaBrenda and her father,
Thomas Weldon Garrett, Sr.

Lnora Garrett Grayson's Children: Dwight, Greg, Glenn, Tony, Christopher, Michael,
and the late Jeffrey Grayson, with sisters, Addie Niles & Wanda Washington

John Hamilton Grant, child of the former **Johnnie Belinda Kennedy** and Dr. John H. **Grant.**

Johnnie Belinda Kennedy Grant, daughter of **John Henry Kennedy** and the former Mary Frances Garlington; married Dr. John H. Grant, and their children are Kontia Jontae and John Hamilton.

Kontia Jontae Grant, child of the former **Johnnie Belinda Kennedy** and Dr. John H. **Grant.**

Anthony Curtis Grayson (b. July 8, 1980) son of **Tony Grayson** and the former Patricia Knight.

Chelsea Grayson (b. Sept. 18, 1990) daughter of **Michael Grayson** and Dierdre.

Christina Grayson (b. May 25, 1988) daughter of **Christopher Francis Grayson** and the former Donna Pierre.

Christopher Francis Grayson (b. Mar. 28, 1967) son of the former (**Missie**) **Lnora Garrett** and Curtis **Grayson;** married the former Donna Pierre, the mother of his two children: son, Damien Curtis, and daughter, Christina.

Corey Grayson (b. Feb. 8, 1978) son of **Michael Grayson** and Jennifer Cadogan.

Damien Curtis Grayson (b. Apr. 3, 1986) son of **Christopher Francis Grayson** and the former Donna Pierre

Dwight Grayson (b. July 26, 1963) son of the former (**Missie**) **Lnora Garrett** and Curtis **Grayson;**

Kevin McNair, Sherona Denny, and their uncle, Dwight Grayson (holding Taylor)

The Rev. Glenn Garrett Grayson & His family

graduated from the Corrections Academy of New York City; lives in New York; married Tenderly Rose Cruz (the daughter of Pedro and Rosa Maria Cruz) and they have had two children, including daughter, Taylor.

The Rev. Glenn Garrett Grayson (b. May 5, 1959) son of the former (**Missie**) **Lnora Garrett** and Curtis **Grayson;** On June 23, 1984, he married the former Marsha Charlene Hughes, (a lawyer, who graduated from Elon College and received Juris Doctor degree in 1986 from the Wake Forest University School of Law) fathering three children: Glenn Garrett Grayson; Shinora, and son, Jeron; graduated from Livingstone College in North Carolina and obtained Master of Divinity degree in 1985 from Hood Theological Seminary in Salisbury, N.C.; maintains

homes in Pittsburgh, Pa. And Hickory Tavern (on land once owned by his great-grandfather, Wick Garrett). Glenn performed the marriage ceremony when his uncle Tom Garrett married Tina.

Glenn Garrett Grayson son of the Rev. **Glenn Garrett Grayson** and the former Marsha Charlene Hughes.

Greg Curtis Grayson (b. Nov. 28, 1960) son of the former (**Missie**) **Lnora Garrett** and Curtis **Grayson;** married the former Hazel Jackson on June 9, 1984, fathering two children: Gregory Curtis Grayson, Jr. and Tamara; graduated from North Carolina Central (after attending Morgan State University where he was a quarterback on the football team); now a member of the Durham Police Department, North Carolina.

Gregory Curtis Grayson, Jr. (b. Apr. 29, 1986) son of **Greg Curtis Grayson** and the former Hazel Jackson.

Jeron Xavier Grayson (b. Apr. 27, 1992) son of the Rev. **Glenn Garrett Grayson** and the former Marsha Hughes.

Latisha Grayson (b. Mar. 30, 1979) daughter of **Tony Grayson** and the former Patricia Knight.

Michael Grayson (b. Sept. 22, 1956) son of the former **Missie Lnora Garrett** and Curtis **Grayson**,; married Dierdre, the mother of his only daughter, Chelsea, and his son, Michael, Jr.; also the father of sons Corey and Kortney; graduated from Technical Career Inst. (A.O.S. electronics).

Kortney Grayson (b. Sept. 24, 1987) son of **Michael Grayson** and Jennifer Cadogan.

Michael Grayson, Jr. (b. July 11, 1995) son of **Michael Grayson** and Dierdre.

(Missie) Lnora Grayson (b. July 4, 1929, Laurens, S.C.) daughter of **Albert Elton Garrett, I and the former Mattie Neely**; married Curtis Grayson (deceased)[47] the father of her nine Children: Jeffrey, Tony, Michael, Ronnie (deceased) Glenn, Gregory Curtis, Wanda Priscilla (Denny, formerly McNair) Dwight, and Christopher Francis; stepdaughter: Addie Grayson Niles (whose children are Brenda and Curtis Niles, and who has a granddaughter named Ashley); resides in Laurens, SC; on July 22, 1995, her children hosted a surprise 66th birthday banquet for her in Brooklyn, New York; it was a joyous family occasion attended by relatives from near and far (including Benjamin Neely, Celeste Harris, Creselene Dakers and her family, Thomas Weldon Garrett, Sr., LaBrenda Garrett-Nelson, Bobby Fletcher Garrett, Regina Neely, and many other family members who reside in the New York area).

Lnora Grayson and her son, Tony

*****Ronnie Grayson** (b. Feb. 23, 1958; d. October 1989) son of the former **(Missie) Lnora** Garrett and Curtis **Grayson**; attended Livingstone College.

Ryan Grayson (b. July 17, 1981) son of Anthony Holt and the former **Wanda Grayson** (see "Denny"); attends North Carolina A&T.

*****Jeffrey Grayson** (b. Aug. 30, 1952; d. Mar. 18, 1996) was the eldest child of the former **(Missie) Lnora Garrett** and Curtis **Grayson**. He received a B.S. degree in accounting from Medgar Evers College, City University of New York, where he also completed further studies in the field of education. At the time of his death, he was teaching at Intermediate School 61 in New York City, as well as

---

4/ Curtis Grayson was the son of Claude Grayson and the former Lelia Grant; he was the brother of Catherine, Claude, Jr., AC, Annabelle, Carol, Jami, and Kenzie.

Dwight, Jeffrey, Ronnie, and Christopher Grayson with sister, Wanda

Jeffrey, Tony, & Michael Grayson

in the Jackie Robinson Program. Jeff attended Public School 167 in Brooklyn, New York, and was honored as an outstanding alumni at the 1995 commencement ceremony. During the Million Man March, in Washington, D.C., in an interview published in the *New York Post* on Oct. 17, 1995, Jeff was quoted as saying "I was taught unity was very important. This is an historical event and I hope it will turn into something good." In addition to his prowess as a mathematician, Jeff was a talented actor. He was a member of the American Theatre of Harlem Ensemble Company and the Black Filmmaker Foundation Acting Ensemble Theatre. His television and film credits include "Law and Order," Spike Lee's "Laughing at the Years," "Smokey Burgess," "Ready or Not," and "Malcolm X." His stage credits include "Back Alley Tales,"

"Raisin in the Sun," and "Blues for Mr. Charlie." He first married (and was widowed by) JoAnn McKinney; married and divorced Gloria (Bonaparte) and Donna (Capers); married the former Leonie Oddman on December 31, 1994; one stepson: Julian.

Shinora Dominique Grayson (b. Feb. 20, 1987) daughter of the Rev. **Glenn Garrett Grayson** and the former Marsha Hughes.

Tamara Grayson (b. Dec. 8, 1985) daughter of **Greg Curtis Grayson** and the former Hazel Jackson.

Tony Grayson (b. Dec. 10, 1953) son of the former **(Missie) Lnora Garrett** and Curtis **Grayson;** first marriage to the former Patricia Knight, the mother of his three children: Yashika, Latisha, and Anthony Curtis; second marriage to Rebecca (mother of his stepson, Steve); attended Queens College, City University of New York; both Tony and Rebecca graduated from Springfield College, Mass., and both are Captains in the NYC Correctional Department; resides in Canarsie, N.Y..

Yashika Grayson (b. Oct. 4, 1973) daughter of **Tony Grayson** and the former Patricia Knight; the mother of Leron Eric Grayson-Allen.

Leron Eric Grayson-Allen (b. Aug. 22, 1995) son of **Yashika Grayson**.

***Daisy Griffin (died in February, 1994 at the age of 105)** daughter of the former **Dicey Garrett (see "Irby")**; mother of Elizabeth W. (Phillips); Cynthia W. (Caldwell); and Herman T. Griffin.[48]

Second cousins: Yashika Grayson and Alexis Garrett Stodghill

Herman T. Griffin, son of **Daisy Griffin**, resident of Greenville, S.C..

Angelica Hansford, daughter of the former **Diane Poole** and Ogden **Hansford**, Sr.

Diane Hansford, daughter of **Odessa Poole**; married Ogden Hansford, the father of her children, Angelica and Ogden, Jr.; a graduate of Clemson University, she is a clinical nurse.

Ogden Hansford, Jr., son of the former **Diane Poole** and Ogden **Hansford**, Sr.

---

[48] Daisy Griffin's daughter, Elizabeth Phillips, reported that Daisy remembered a "grandpa Benham" who was an Irishman.

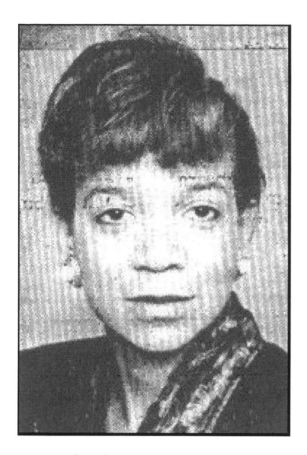

Abigail Ramona Rogers Harris

Judge Abigail Ramona Rogers Harris (b. 1957) daughter of the former **Shelly Ruth Garrett (now Kimpson)** and Willie Robert Rogers; married to Fred Allen Harris (First Sergeant, U.S. Army) on Sept. 21, 1991, the father of her daughter: Garrett Ella; 1982 graduate of the University of South Carolina School of Law; served as the resident Judge of the Fifth Judicial Circuit Family Court in Richland and Kershaw counties. She was the first (and to date, only) African American woman elected to the judgeship on a statewide basis by the South Carolina General Assembly. Abigail was a victim of the historic, nationwide Republican victory in the 1994 mid-term elections; Republicans who gained power in the South Carolina legislature railroaded her out of office. She bore her replacement by a white female Republican with dignity and grace, and the family remains very proud of her achievements.

Clifford Harris, Jr., son of the former **Patricia Ann** Latimer and Clifford **Harris.**

Crystal Renea Harris, daughter of the former **Patricia Ann** Latimer and Clifford **Harris.**

Darrell Harris, daughter of the former **Patricia Ann** Latimer and Clifford **Harris.**

Garrett Ella Harris (b. 1994) daughter of the former **Abigail Ramona Rogers** and Fred **Harris.**

Patricia Ann Harris, daughter of the former **Ruby Williams** and Charlie Walker **Latimer;** married Clifford Harris, the father of Tonya Shawn, Darrell, Clifford, Jr., and Crystal Renea.

Tonya Shawn Harris, daughter of the former **Patricia Ann** Latimer and Clifford **Harris.**

Rita Henderson, daughter of the former **Mildred Beasley** and David **Young;** married with one daughter.

Beverly Marie Henessee, daughter of **Juanita K. Henessee** and Ford Henessee.

Juanita K. Henessee, daughter of the former **Mamie Garrett** and Henry **Kennedy;** married Ford Henessee, and her children are Beverly Marie and William Ford.

William Ford Henessee, son of **Juanita K. Henessee** and Ford Henessee.

Ashley Elaine Hunter (b. Feb. 25, 1991) daughter of the former **Marye Elaine Boston** and Kevin **Hunter;** goddaughter of LaBrenda Garrett-Nelson.

Jason Hunter (b. May 27, 1986) son of the former **Marye Elaine Boston** and Kevin **Hunter;** godson of LaBrenda Garrett-Nelson.

1982: (Seated) Michael Grayson, Desiree Durden, and (Standing) Javan Boston, Jr., Marye Elaine Hunter, and Tony Grayson

Ashley Hunter

(**Marye**) **Elaine Hunter** (b. Dec. 6, 1953, Laurens, S.C.) daughter of the former **Frances Garrett** and Javan **Boston**, Sr.; married Kevin Nick Hunter (who graduated from the State University of New York at New Paul College[49]) the father of her two children: Jason and Ashley Elaine; graduated from Lander College in S.C.; she is a Delta; former teacher, resident in Mauldin, S.C..

***Dicey Irby** (b. Laurens, S.C.; d.) daughter of **Ike and Hannah Garrett**; married twice to Mr. Johnson and Lee Irby (a man who had been owned by a Colonel Irby[50]); the mother of Daisy (Griffin); Mary; James; and Pearl (Dakers).

***Gab Irby** (d.) daughter of **James Irby, Sr.**.

***Grace Lee B. Irby** daughter of the former **Early Garrett** and Crockett **Beasley**. She was a prime mover in organizing the Church of God in Laurens.

***James ("Jim") Irby**, son of the former **Dicey Garrett** and Lee **Irby**; he had a shop on "back street" in Laurens, where he repaired washing machines; the father of James, Jr. and two daughters, Sipy and Gab (both deceased).[51]

---

[49] Kevin Hunter is the only child of the former Joyce Berry (now Bronstroph) and Alonzo Nick Hunter.
[50] SOURCE: John Dakers
[51] SOURCES: John Dakers and Thomas W. Garrett, Sr.

Cousins, Jim Irby and Lucius Dakers (1996)

James Irby, Jr. ("Buggy") son of **James Irby;** he is a minister in the Jehovah's Witnesses and resides in New York; he has a son.

James Marion Irby (b. Nov. 26, 1918) son of **Pearl Irby Dakers**, resides in Stockbridge, Ga.

* **Mary Irby** (d.) daughter of **Ike and Hannah Garrett.**

* **Wilamehnia** ("Sipy") **Irby** (d.) daughter of **James Irby, Sr.**.

Anne Jeffcoat, daughter of **A.C. Garrett.**

Raquel Jefferson, daughter of **Linda Lynch.**

Marjorie Johnson, the eighth child of **Willie Jackson Beasley** and the former Katie Annette Wilson; married Calvin Johnson; graduated from Benedict College and did graduate work at NYU and Howard University; taught for 33 years in the public schools of Laurens County; now resides in Simpsonville, S.C.

Martha Kennedy Jones, daughter of the former **Mamie Garrett** and Henry **Kennedy**; she married Darryl Jones and their children are Keisha and Rita.

Anjelica Kennedy, daughter of **Mike Kennedy.**

Barbara Denise Kennedy, daughter of **Cyril Wade Kennedy** and Alfreda.

Callie Kennedy, son of the former **Mamie Garrett** and Henry **Kennedy**; married Martha, and they had three daughters.

Christopher Poitier Kennedy, adopted son of **John Henry Kennedy** and the former Mary Frances Garlington; the birth son of Betty Ruth Kennedy Calivile.

Cid Kennedy, son of **David Michael Kennedy** and the former Lula Mae Hooker.

Cyril Wade Kennedy, son of **Garrett Kennedy** and the former Wilhelmina Cleveland; married Alfreda, and their children are Barbara Denise and Cyril, Jr.

Cyril Wade Kennedy, Jr., son of **Cyril Wade Kennedy** and Alfreda.

David Michael Kennedy, son of **Garrett Kennedy** and the former Wilhelmina Cleveland; married Lula Mae Hooker; the father of Cid Kennedy and Ivan Kennedy.

The Rev. David Kennedy (b. 1952) son **of John Henry Kennedy** and the former Francis Garlington; married the former Janet Presley (she graduated from Lander College and received graduate degree from Peabody in Tennessee); graduated from Benedict College and both he and his wife did graduate work in Tennessee. A community activist, he is the pastor of New Beginnings Baptist Missionary, where he operates the only soup kitchen in Laurens.

He and his wife are the parents of three children: Lola, Dieja, and Lorenzo.

Dieja Kennedy, son of **the Rev. David Kennedy** and the former Janet Presley. He is a student at Laurens High where he is a basketball teammate of his fifth cousin, Albert Garrett, III.

*****Garrett Kennedy,** son of the former **Mamie Garrett** and Henry **Kennedy**; married the former Wilhelmina Cleveland; their children are Jacqueline (Pruitt) Ronald Bernard, Cyril Wade, and David Michael.

Ivan Kennedy, son of **David Michael Kennedy** and the former Lula Mae Hooker.

(Willie) J. Kennedy, son of the former **Mamie Garrett** and Henry **Kennedy**; married Ruth; had four children.

John Henry Kennedy, son of **Mamie Kennedy**; married the former Francis Garlington, the mother of his children: the Rev. David Kennedy, and daughters Belinda and Pamela; also adopted three children: Christopher Poitier Kennedy (the birth son of Betty Ruth Kennedy Calivile); Jacqueta LaShea Kennedy (Mills) and Tya L. (both are birth daughters of Saundra Kennedy Young).

Leroy Kennedy, son of the former **Mamie Garrett** and **Henry Kennedy**; the father of Sandra (Young).

Lola Kennedy, daughter of **the Rev. David Kennedy** and the former Janet Presley.

Lorenzo Kennedy, son **of the Rev. David Kennedy** and the former Janet Presley.

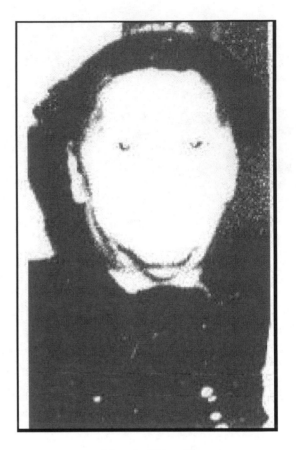

Mamie Kennedy

*****Mamie Garrett Martin Kennedy** (b. December 1891, Laurens, S.C.; d.) daughter of **Samuel M. Garrett** and the former Hattie Hunter; married Toy Martin, the father of Samuel Martin, Sonny Boy Martin, and Odessa Martin (Poole), and then married John Henry Kennedy. The father of sons, Garrett, Callie, Leroy, John Henry, and Willie J., and daughters, Juanita K. (Hennesse) and Sallie . She attended South Carolina State College Mamie and Henry are buried at Flat Ruff Baptist Church.[52]

---

[52] SOURCES: Thomas W. Garrett, Sr.; Frances Boston; Saundra Kennedy Young, and Lillie Williams-Tims. John Henry Kennedy also had four children by his first wife: Cora Goodjoin Kennedy; Aliene Kennedy Johnson (who married Fred, the father of Cora who married William Molloy); Emanuel Kennedy (who married Vera), Louise Kennedy Campbell (who married Callie, the father of Cora Kennedy Owens), and Ida Mell (?) Kennedy Humbert (who married Frank).

Marian Kennedy Jones, daughter of **William James Kennedy** and the former Ruth Workman; married Willie Jones; she is the mother of Mike Kennedy.

Marion Kennedy, son of **William James Kennedy** and the former Ruth Workman.

Michael David Kennedy, son of the former Wilhelmina Cleveland and **Garrett Kennedy**.

Mike Kennedy, the son of **Marian Kennedy Jones;** the father of Anjelica Kennedy.

Ralph Ira Kennedy (died at age 7), son of **John Henry Kennedy** and the former Mary Frances Garlington.

Ronald Bernard Kennedy, son of the former Wilhelmina Cleveland and **Garrett Kennedy**.

Sallie Kennedy, daughter of Garrett Kennedy and the former Wilhelmina Cleveland; died at an early age.

OWEN RILEY JR. / Staff

Applause: *The Rev. Jesse Jackson's comments about the Klan in Laurens bring applause Monday from ministers and others sharing the podium with him at the New Beginnings Missionary Baptist Church in Laurens.*

Help close Redneck Shop, Jesse Jackson urges Reno

By April E. Moorefield
LAURENS BUREAU

LAURENS — The Rev. Jesse Jackson called on the U.S. Justice Department to investigate whether the owner of a store that sells and displays Ku Klux Klan material is violating the civil rights of African-Americans.

Jackson said his goal is to shut down the shop. Addressing about 100 people who gathered at a local church Monday, the civil rights leader said he asked Attorney General Janet Reno to send representatives to Laurens to conduct the probe.

"Our goal is to close it down, and more than that, destroy the fear, terrorism and hatred it represents," Jackson said. "The good news is that black and white citizens

are already standing up and fighting back. There is an ugly mood in the world, and people of good will must fight back."

"Any acts of intimidation or violence that might serve to harm or violate civil rights must be stopped. What is at stake is our dignity, and our dignity isn't negotiable. I am awaiting her response," he said, referring to Reno.

A Justice Department official wouldn't comment publicly Monday on Jackson's request.

Meanwhile, the owner of The Redneck Shop, which has captured the national spotlight in recent weeks with its billing as the "World's Only KKK Museum," said he eventually will display only Confederate

See **SHOP** on page **4A**

OWEN RILEY JR. / Staff

Shop owner: *John Howard meets reporters Monday in his Redneck Shop in Laurens.*

FROM THE GREENVILLE NEWS, Mar. 19, 1996: The Rev. David Kennedy (a great-grandson of Samuel M. Garrett) to the right of the Rev. Jesse Jackson, at the church where David serves as Pastor.

Tya L. Kennedy, adopted daughter of **John Henry Kennedy** and the former Mary Frances Garlington; birth daughter of Saundra Kennedy Young.

Willie James Kennedy (d. 1998), son of the former **Mamie Garrett** and Henry **Kennedy;** married the former Ruth Workman, the mother of Betty Ruth (Colville); Willie James, Jr., and Marion, Marian.

Willie James Kennedy, Jr., son of **William James Kennedy** and the former Ruth Workman; married Azalee.

Shelly Ruth Rogers Kimpson (b. 1933, Laurens, S.C.) daughter of **Shellie Donaldson Garrett** and the former Alberta Barksdale; widowed from marriage to Wilbur Rogers, the father of her two children: Abigail Ramona (Harris) and Wilfred Garrett; second marriage to Joe Kimpson; graduated from Benedict College; now resident in Columbia, S.C..

Carlos Latimer, son of the former **Ruby Williams** and Charlie Walker **Latimer.**

Charles Latimer, son of the former **Ruby Williams** and Charlie Walker **Latimer;** married the former Pauline Bunny McKee, the mother of Raydale, Eric, and Dalvon.

Dalvon Latimer, son of **Charles Latimer** and the former Pauline Bunny McKee

Eric Latimer, son of **Charles Latimer** and the former Pauline Bunny McKee

Lisa Latimer, daughter of the former **Ruby Williams** and Charlie Walker **Latimer.**

Phyllis Latimer, daughter of **Willie Harold Garrett** and the former Lela Thompson (now Jenkins); she married and had three children: sons, LaMont and Twins one of whom died in infancy.

Raydale Latimer, child of **Charles Latimer** and the former Pauline Bunny McKee.

Theresa Latimer, daughter of the former **Ruby Williams** and Charlie Walker **Latimer.**

Ruby Latimer, daughter of the former **Carrie Lee Garrett** and Hunter Nathaniel **Williams,** Sr.; married Charlie Walker Latimer, the father of her children: Charles, Patricia Ann (Harris) Carol (Anderson) Theresa, Lisa Lynette, and Carlos Britt.

Chandra Lloyd (b. Dec. 26, 1993) daughter of **William L. Lloyd** and the former Kim Herbin.

Clifton H. Lloyd, Jr., son of the former **Lila Garrett** and Clifton **Lloyd;** attended the NC School of the Arts for three years and played with various bands, including the Greensboro Youth Orchestra, Winston Salem Symphony, and UNC-G Jazz Band. He is currently employed with Cox Transportation Company.

Sisters, Shelly Ruth Kimpson & Lila Garrett Lloyd, with first cousin, Thomas Weldon Garrett, Sr.

Lila Garrett Lloyd (b. Mar. 10, 1937, Laurens, S.C.; Twin to: Lillian who died six days after birth) daughter of **Shellie Donaldson Garrett** and the former Alberta Barksdale; married Clifton Lloyd, Sr. (who received a B.A. in instrumental music from NC A&T State University, and an M.A. in the same subject from Indiana University; retired as a Music Educator from the Chatham County School system; has previously taught in August, Ga., Bath, SC, Howard County, MD., and Siler City, NC), the father of her two sons: William Penn and Clifton, Jr.; she is a former teacher in the Guilford County School system, and is currently an instructor at NC A&T State University in the Department of Business and Economics. She is active in the community and has served as past president of the Friends of the Library, Woodbriar Avenue and Neighbors Club, and the American Association of University Women. She also led a coalition to establish the McGirt-Horton Library in her neighborhood, and is a member of the Delta Sigma Theta Sorority.

Lila obtained a B.A. from Benedict College, a M. Ed. From the University of North Carolina at Greensboro, and a Ph. D. from Columbia Pacific University. She is a member of the Laughlin Memorial United Methodist Church, where she is an Adult Sunday School teacher. She has received many awards for her service to the community.

William Penn Lloyd (b. June 9, 1961) son of the former **Lila Garrett** and Clifton **Lloyd**; graduated from North Carolina A & T in Greensboro with a B.A. in music, and obtained an M.A. in Admin. And Supervision from Bowie State University; married the former Kim Herbin, the mother of his daughter: Chandra; he is a teacher at Bladensburg High School in Maryland, and the Band Director and TV Production teacher.

Erica Logan, daughter of the former **(Martha) Phyllis Wade** and Eric Logan.

(Martha) Phyllis Wade Logan (b. 1949) daughter of the former **Josephine Simons** and George W. **Wade**; married and divorced Eric Logan; graduated from Roberts Wesleyan; Masters degree from University of Rochester; currently the Dean of Students at the Eastman School of Music, University of Rochester; mother of Phillip and Erica.

Phillip Logan, son of the former **(Martha) Phyllis Wade** and Eric **Logan**.

Darrell Lynch, son of the former **Mamie Lee Beasley** and Ernest **Lynch**; father of Shondrell and Nicole.

Gilbert Lynch, son of the former **Mamie Lee Beasley** and Ernest **Lynch**; a photographer with a shop in Fountain Inn, S.C.; he resides in Greenville, S.C.; father of Renisha and Vontray.

Keith Lynch, son of the former **Mamie Beasley** and Ernest **Lynch**; father of Keith, Jr..

Keith Lynch, Jr., son of **Keith Lynch**.

Linda Lynch, daughter of the former **Mamie Lee Beasley** and Ernest **Lynch**; mother of Raquel Jefferson.

***Mamie Lee Beasley Lynch** (b. May 25, 1921, d. Laurens, S.C.) daughter of **Willie Jackson Beasley** and the former Katie Annette Wilson; married Ernest Lynch (a retired postal worker, and now a photographer, from Chicago — he took the official photographs at the 1994 GNS reunion); Ernest is the father of her sons, Darrell, Gilbert, Keith, and Frederick, and her daughter, Linda; she attended Benedict College and taught at the Oak Grove Community School from 1945-49; she also served as a substitute teacher at Baker Coffee Elementary school in Lexington, S.C..

Nicole Lynch, daughter of **Darrell Lynch**.

Renisha Lynch, daughter of **Gilbert Lynch**.

Shondrell Lynch, daughter of **Darrell Lynch**.

Vontray Lynch, daughter of **Gilbert Lynch**.

***Cora Altamease Lyons** (b. Laurens, S.C.; d. 1997) daughter of **C.D. Beasley and M.L. Neely**; attended Florida A&M and Clark; first married Robert Gilder, then Rufus Lyons of Laurens, S.C.; resident of Tampa, Florida; the namesake of Altamease (Sullivan) Culver.

Edward Herbert Mack, Jr. (b. July 7, 1975) son of the former **Denise Garrett** (see "Fredericks") and the late Edward Herbert Mack.[53]

Michelle Martin, daughter of the former **Sharyn Tucker** (see "McCalla") and her first husband, Wendell Martin; graduated from Hofstra University.

Lauren McCalla (b. July 5, 1984) daughter of the former **Sharyn** Tucker and Michael **McCalla**.

Shaniece McCalla (b. Oct. 27, 1982) daughter of the former **Sharyn** Tucker and Michael **McCalla**

---

[53] Edward Mack, Sr. was the son of the late Osborn Mack (a native of Lexington County, S.C.) and the former Evelyn Webb (from New Jersey); his siblings were Giovanni, James Osborne, Alvin Richard, Marvin Nathaniel, David Leonard, Michael Thomas, John Henry, Osborne Albert, James Emmanuel, Alfred, and Michael, and a sister, Marie. The legendary singer, Sam Cooke, was a Mack cousin.

First Cousins: Demaunt Robinson, Edward Mack,
and Alexis Garrett Stodghill

Mr. And Mr. Frank McDowell

.**Sharyn McCalla** (b. Feb. 18, 1948) eldest child of the former **Mattie Elton Garrett** and Edward Jordan **Tucker**, Sr.; married first to Wendell Martin, the father of her daughter, Michelle, and then to Michael McCalla, the father of two other daughters: Lauren and Shaniece; graduated from Wagner College on Staten Island, N.Y.

Ethel McDowell ("**Toots**") daughter of the former Evelyn Hill and **Willie Edgar Beasley**; married Frank McDowell; resides in Laurens, S.C.

Allie Marie McDuffie (b. Dec. 11, 1941) daughter of the former **Alma** Yeargins and Henry **Summers**; married Robert McDuffie, the father of her two daughters, Alma Lisa and Robin Kimiko.

Alma Lisa McDuffie (b. Dec. 15, 1975) daughter of the former **Allie** Summers and Robert **McDuffie;** attends Clemson University.

Robin Kimiko McDuffie (b. July 1, 1966) daughter of the former **Allie** Summers and Robert **McDuffie,** a graduate of Clemson University

Kevin McNair, Jr., son of the former **Wanda Grayson** (see "Denny") and her first husband, Kevin McNair.

Hattie Milan daughter of **Ike and Hannah Garrett**

Jacqueta LaShea Mills; adopted daughter of **John Henry Kennedy** and the former Mary Frances Garlington; birth daughter of Saundra Kennedy Young; married Larry Mills, Jr., and they have a son.

Clara Moody, daughter of **Garfield Beasley** and the former Clara Floyd; resident of Baltimore, Md.

Corrine Ruth Nicholson (b. July 11, 1991) daughter of **William Garrett Nicholson** and the former Jennifer Dreyfus.

David Emanuel Nicholson (b. 1951) son of the former **Ruth Simons** and Louis Roy **Nicholson**; graduated from the Sidwell Friends School in Washington, D.C.; attended Haverford College before obtaining degree from the University of the District of Columbia; masters in fine arts from the University of Iowa; assistant editor of "Book World" of Washington Post; editor of **Black Film Review**, a magazine founded in 1985.

Elena Rebecca Nicholson (b. Mar. 30, 1995) daughter of **William Garrett Nicholson** and the former Jennifer Dreyfus.

Alexis Garrett Stodghill with her fifth cousin, Corrine Ruth Nicholson (in arms) and her fourth cousin, once removed, Josephine Nicholson, outside Bethel Hall in 1994

Josephine Monica Nicholson (b. 1954) daughter of the former **Ruth Simons** and Louis Roy **Nicholson**; obtained masters degree in dance education from George Washington University; graduated from Wilson College in Penn.; married Timothy Carter Brown, on Dec. 3, 1994.

Dr. Phyllis Elizabeth Nicholson, M.D. (b. 1953) daughter of the former **Ruth Simons** and Louis Roy **Nicholson**; graduated from the University of Maryland Medical School in 1982; married David Williams, the father of her daughter Nia Endesha Halima.

*Ruth Esther Simons Nicholson (b. Nov. 22, 1922; d. Aug. 26, 1986); daughter of the former **Mattie**

Phyllis Garrett and Alfred **Simons;** married Louis Roy Nicholson (divorced in 1960, a native of Jamaica; a dentist who graduated from Howard University) producing four children: David Emanuel: William Garrett: Josephine Monica; and Phyllis Elizabeth; graduated from Howard University and obtained masters degree in the humanities from the University of Chicago—a Delta, Ruth was a teacher before becoming a librarian; she retired from the Library of Congress.

William Garrett Nicholson (b. 1959) son of the former **Ruth Simons** and Louis Roy **Nicholson** (a dentist); He is a lawyer who attended Georgetown University Law Center (after graduating from Tufts) and passed the bar in 1988. He married the former Jennifer Dreyfus on Oct. 3, 1987, the mother of his two daughters: Corinne Ruth and Elena Rebecca.

Elizabeth W. Phillips, daughter of **Daisy Griffin**, resident of Fort Washington, Md.

Odessa M. Poole, daughter of the former **Mamie Garrett Kennedy**; married; one daughter named Diane (Hansford); a classroom teacher in Laurens County who taught many of her younger Garrett cousins.

Evangeline Price ("Bango") (b. May 31, 1949; TWIN to Madeline); daughter of the former **Mattie Elton Garrett** and Edward Jordan **Tucker**, Sr.; married and divorced Charles Price; two children: Nicole and Christopher Durham.

Nicole Price, daughter of the former **Evangeline Tucker** and Charles **Price**; mother of Derrell Brown, Anthony Brown, Naajia Benjamin, and Tyrone Benjamin.

Jacqueline Kennedy Pruitt, daughter of the former Wilhelmina Cleveland and **Garrett Kennedy**; married.

Angela Rampage, daughter of the former **Eunice Garrett** and Willie **Ramage**.

Anthony Ramage, son of the former **Eunice Garrett** and Willie **Ramage.**

Eunice Ramage, daughter of Mag and **Chester Garrett**; married Willie Ramage; their children are Mary Joe (Walker) Angela, and Anthony.

Dr. A Garrett Ridgley, Sr., whose mother was a Garrett, attended Howard University; a cousin remembered by Josephine Simons Wade; he is listed as a 1947 graduate in the Howard University Alumni Directory (although his name appears with a star, indicating that they had been unable to locate him); Josephine also remembered that he had a daughter and (apparently, a son named after him).

Demaunt, Robin, and Mahdisiah (2000)

Demaunt Shannon Robinson (**"Prince"**) (b. Oct. 21, 1975) son of **Jacqueline Garrett** and Don Robinson; attended North Carolina A&T; has also done part-time acting and modeling; graduated from the Art Institute of Atlanta in 1997; the father of a son, Mahdisiah Shallah El-Khaalik, whose mother is Robin Wu.

Prince (1997)

Mahdisiah Shallah El-khaalik (b. Oct. 4, 1999), son of **Demaunt Shannon Robinson ("Prince")** and Robin Wu ("China").

Wilfred Garrett Rogers, son of **the former Shelly Ruth Garrett** (see "Kimpson"); married the former Pamela Foster; graduated from Benedict College in 1983; masters in education from University of South Carolina in 1993.

Bridjet Russell (b. July 26, 1991; TWIN to Brittni) daughter of **Teresa Garrett**.

Brittni Russell (b. July 26, 1991 ; TWIN to Bridjet) daughter of **Teresa Garrett**.

Rosalyn Salters, daughter of the former **Ruth Williams** and Rosco **Stoddard**; married Ray A. Salters.

***Tildy Sexton** (b. Laurens, S.C.) daughter of **Ike and Hannah Garrett**; married twice to Mr. Austin and Mr. Sexton.

Kayla Shaw (b. June 2, 1986) daughter of **Javan Boston, Jr.** And Sandra Shaw.

Cardell Elisha Shortt, son of the former **Carolyn Beasley** and Robert Elisha **Shortt**; the Administrator for Beasley's Home For The Aged.

Carolyn Yvonne Shortt, daughter of **C.D. Beasley** and the former Lucinda Sherman; she married Robert Elisha Shortt,[54] whom she met at Johnson C. Smith College, on May 28, 1968 in the Church of God, Laurens. Bob retired as Assistant Superintendent of Student Personnel Services for Laurens County School District No. 55, and was formerly principal of Pleasant View Primary School. Carolyn is the Director of Parenting for Laurens County School District No. 55, and serves on the Board of Trustees of Frances Marion University. They are the parents of Cardell Elisha and Robert Beasley.

Robert Beasley Shortt, son of the former **Carolyn Beasley** and Robert Elisha **Short**; now attending Lander University.

Dr. Alfred Edgar Simons, Jr. (Ph.D.) (b. Feb. 14, 1919) son of the former **Mattie Phyllis Garrett** and Alfred **Simons**; graduated from Miner Teachers College; was the leader of the 357th Engineers Band and served in World War II; obtained doctorate at Columbia University; teacher; was a professor at Prince Georges Community College in Maryland; first married and (after 25 years) divorced the former Marion Lee Moody (mother of his sons: Alfred, III

---

[54] Bob was born in Richmond Virginia to Elisha Shortt and the former Thelma Boyd; he grew up in Lawrenceville, Va..

The Power of a Good Teacher City Councilman H.E. Crawford (right) and his sixth-grade teacher, Dr. Alfred Simons, now at Prince George's Community College.

FROM THE WASHINGTONIAN

and Steven); second marriage to Princess Josephine Campbell.

Alfred Edgar Simons, III (b. 1949) son of **Alfred Edgar Simons, Jr.** and the former Marion Lee Moody.

Casper Garrett Simons (b. Oct. 16, 1920) son of the former **Mattie Phyllis Garrett** and Alfred **Simons**, retired postal worker; resides in New Jersey; two sons: Casper, Jr. And Paul Anthony; one adoptive daughter, (Beatrice) Olivia; married three times (after deaths of first two wives): first to the former Vivian Craig (mother of Casper, Jr.); then to the former Pauline Dinkins (mother of Paul Anthony); and then to the former Laurena Olivia (mother of his stepdaughter, Beatrice, whom Casper, Sr. adopted).

Casper Garrett Simons, Jr. (b. 1940) son of **Casper Garrett Simons** and the former Vivian Craig.

*Daryl Simons (b. 1960;, TWIN to Douglas) son of **Kemble Taylor Simons** and the former Johnnie Smith.

Delrico Simons, adoptive son (and grandson) of **Kemble Taylor Simons** and natural child of Kevin Simons; a senior at Michigan State.

Douglas Simons (b. 1960; TWIN to Daryl) son of **Kemble Taylor Simons** and the former Johnnie Smith.

Jon Myron Simons (b. 1961) son of **Kemble Taylor Simons** and the former Johnnie Smith; graduated from the U.S. Naval Academy at Annapolis in 1982.

Kemble Taylor Simons (b. 1928) son of the former **Mattie Phyllis Garrett** and Alfred **Simons**; electrical engineering degree from Howard University; served in the U.S. Navy (radar technician); now resides in Cincinnati, Ohio; married Johnnie Mae Smith (a widow who had two children: Michael and Vanessa, both of whom were adopted by Kemble); four sons were born of this marriage: Jon Myron; Twins: Douglas and Daryl (deceased) and Kevin; also adopted Kevin's son, Delrico.

Kevin Simons (b. 1956) son of **Kemble Taylor Simons** and the former Johnnie Smith; attended Yale University; biological father of Delrico Simons.

*Mattie Phyllis (christened "Martha") Simons (b. June 18, 1891; d. July 10, 1959) daughter of **Casper George Garrett** and the former Anna M. Threewitts; married Alfred Edgar Simons (who attended Benedict College[55]) the father of her eight children: Josephine (Wade); Alfred; Casper Garrett; Ruth (Nicholson); William; Phyllis Threewitts (Ferguson); Kemble Taylor; and Mills McDaniel— all three of Mattie's daughters married dentists; Mattie was the first female graduate of the College Department of Allen University, where she taught before marriage.

Michael Simons, son of **Kemble Taylor Simons** and the former Johnnie Smith.

Mills McDaniel Simons ("Mac") (b. 1931) son of the former **Mattie Phyllis Garrett** and Alfred **Simons**; attended Miner Teachers College; retired from Howard University.

Paul Anthony Simons (b.1945) son of **Casper Garrett Simons, Sr.** and the former Pauline Dinkins; graduated from Park College in Missouri; retired Air Force Captain, now residing in Cincinnati, Ohio; first marriage to Charlotte, mother of his daughter, Shannon.

Shannon Simons, daughter of **Paul Anthony Simons** and Charlotte, his first wife.

Sheryl Patrice Simons (b. 1954) daughter **of William Henry Simons, II** and the former Elaine Valeria Davis; New York University graduate who lives in Philadelphia.

Steven Simons (b. 1955) son of **Alfred Edgar Simons, Jr.** and the former Marion Lee Moody; paralegal.

William H. Simons son of the former **Mattie Phyllis Garrett** and Alfred **Simons**; graduated from Miner Teachers College and obtained a masters degree from New York University; the first president of the Washington, D.C. Teachers Union, an elected position that he held for 20 years (see May 20, 1981 Washington Post article) and a vice president of the American Federation of Teachers; served as the D.C. State Democratic chairperson; his family is very proud of his work with the labor movement in South Africa; married Elaine Valeria Davis (retired junior high school counselor; Miner Teachers College and graduate work at the University of Pennsylvania before obtaining masters from American University) producing two daughters: Sheryl Patrice and Wilma Lorraine.

---

[55] Alfred Edgar Simons (1883-1956) was one of the twelve children of Isom Wesley (1849-1914) and Minnie Josephine (1863-1927) Simons of Columbia, S.C.; Isom was the son of William Henry (1819-1880) and Fannie Syrene (1819-1887) Simons; and William Henry was the son of John Washington (d. 1899) and Mary Simons; additional information about the Simons can be found in the "Red Book," by Alfred Edgar's sister, Minnie Simons Williams: **A Colloquial History of a Black South Carolina Family Named Simons** (1990).

The family of Alfred E. Simons, Sr., and his wife Mattie P. Simons, 1944. **Front row, from left:** Ruth Esther Simons, Anna Josephine Simons, Casper Garrett Simons, Jr., Mattie P. Simons, Phyllis Threewitts Simons. Alfred E. Simons, Sr. is seated behind Phyllis. **Standing:** Alfred E. Simons, Jr., William Henry Simons, Kemble Taylor Simons; Casper Garret Simons, Sr.; Mills McDaniel (Mac) Simons.

Mayor Barry; William Simons, Washington Teachers Union; Albert Shanker (rear), American Federation of Teachers the

Rev. Ernest R. Gibson, head of the D.C. Coalition Against Tuition Tax Credits, and Del. Walter Fauntroy celebrate victory.

By Craig Herndon—The Washington Post

FROM THE WASHINGTON POST,
May 20, 1981

Wilma Lorraine Simons (b. 1963) daughter of **William Henry Simons, II** and the former Elaine Valeria Davis; graduate of Georgetown University; MBA from Georgia Tech; works for Georgia Pacific; now resides in Atlanta, Ga..

Caroline Smith, daughter of **Moses Smith** and the former Mamie Smith.

Chanel Rose Smith (b. 1984) granddaughter of **Dorothy Dakers Smith.**

Damien Andre Smith (b. 1980) grandson of **Dorothy Dakers Smith.**

Dorothy Dakers Smith and grandchild

Moses Smith

Dorothy Dakers Smith ("Baby Rose") (b. Feb. 10, 1934, Clinton, S.C.) daughter of **Lucius Warren Dakers** and the late Rosa Lee Moore; married John Wesley Smith, the father of her four children: Martha (White) Wesley, Warren Dakers, and William Powell; graduated valedictorian of Bell Street High School and matriculated at North Carolina College, in Durham, N.C.; obtained B.S. in education from Temple University, and attended graduate school at University of Pennsylvania, Wharton School of Social Work; resident of Philadelphia, Penn..

***Early Smith** (b. Sept. 15, 1891; d. Apr. 17, 1954) daughter of **Wick Garrett** and the former Frances Latimer; married Henry Smith (b. June 18, 1873; d. May 19, 1955); one son: Moses; she was a college graduate who worked as a nurse in New York.

Moses Smith, son of **the former Early Garrett** and Henry **Smith;** he married the former Mamie Smith of Laurens County, and they had a son, Moses, Jr., and a daughter named Caroline; he died in New York.

Moses Smith, Jr., son of **Moses Smith** and the former Mamie Smith.

Tiffany Alaia Smith (b. 1986) granddaughter of **Dorothy Dakers Smith.**

Warren Dakers Smith (b. Sept. 23, 1958) son of the former **Dorothy Dakers** and John Wesley **Smith;** married to Doreen; resident of Bear, Delaware.

Wesley Constantino Smith (b. Mar. 15, 1957) son of the former **Dorothy Dakers** and John Wesley **Smith;** married to Dayra; resident of Harrisburg, Penn..

William Powell Smith (b. Feb. 16, 1983) son of the former **Dorothy Dakers** and John Wesley **Smith.**

Allen Stoddard, son of the former **Catherine Williams** and Larry **Stoddard;** married the former Maddie Mosely; their children are Terance, Tonia, and Tiffany.

Brandon Antwan Stoddard, son of **Larry Reggie Stoddard.**

*(Hattie Mae) **Catherine Stoddard** (b. May 17; d. 1994) daughter of the former **Carrie Lee Garrett** and Hunter Nathaniel **Williams,** Sr.; married Larry M. Stoddard, Sr. (part of the same family as her sister Ruth's husband) the father of her sons: Allen, Jackie, Larry, Diroger (died in infancy) and Therin.[56]

Catherine Shun Stoddard, daughter of **Stevie Stoddard.**

Chelsey Shuntay Stoddard, daughter of **Stevie Stoddard.**

Jackie Stoddard, son of the former **Catherine Williams** and Larry **Stoddard,** Sr.

Kristy Shalanie Stoddard, daughter of **Stevie Stoddard.**

Larry M. Stoddard, Jr. son of the former **Catherine Williams** and Larry **Stoddard;** married the former Betty Allen, the mother of Stevie, Vern Lamont, Rosalyn Venessa, and Larry Reggie.

Larry Reggie Stoddard, son of **Larry Stoddard,** Jr. and the former Betty Allen; the father of Brandon Antwan Stoddard.

Markese Rashad Stoddard, child of **Rosalyn Venessa Stoddard.**

Patrick Therin Stoddard, son of the former Jannette Jones Pulley and **Therin Stoddard, Sr.**

Rosalyn Stoddard, daughter of the former **Ruth Williams** and Rosco **Stoddard.**

Rosalyn Venessa Stoddard, daughter of **Larry M. Stoddard, Jr.** and the former Betty Allen; mother of Markese Rashad.

Ruth Stoddard, daughter of the former **Carrie Lee Garrett** and Hunter Nathaniel **Williams,** Sr.; married Rosco Stoddard (part of the same family as her sister Catherine's husband) the father of Venessa and Rosalyn.

Stevie Stoddard, son of **Larry M. Stoddard, Jr.,** and the former Betty Allen; the father of Catherine Shun, Kristy Shuntay, and Chelsey Shalanie.

Terance Stoddard, son of **Allen Stoddard** and the former Maddie Mosely.

Tiffany Alana Stoddard, daughter of **Allen Stoddard** and the former Maddie Mosely.

Tonia Stoddard, daughter of **Allen Stoddard** and the former Maddie Mosely.

Therin Stoddard, Sr., son of the former **Catherine Williams** and Larry **Stoddard;** married the former Jannetta Jones Pulley; his children are Patrick Therin and Therin Stoddard, Jr..

Therin Stoddard, Jr., son of **Therin Stoddard, Sr.** and the former Jannette Jones Pulley.

Vern Lamont Stoddard, son of **Larry M. Stoddard, Jr.** and the former Betty Allen.

---

[11] SOURCE: Catherine Stoddard's half-sister, Lillie Williams-Tims of the African American Historical Foundation of Laurens, South Carolina.

Alexis Garrett Stodghill (born Alexis Garrett Bowman[57] on Nov. 11, 1973, adopted by mother's second husband, Charles Stodghill) daughter of **LaBrenda Garrett-Nelson**; graduated from the Sidwell Friends School in Washington, D.C.; after taking a year off to intern for the U.S. Congress, Joint Tax Committee; she graduated from Brown University in 1996.

Alexis Garrett Bowman Stodghill

She is a new media professional, who has worked as a (web) Site Editor at agency.com, as an assistant producer at Fortune.com, and is now a Senior Product Producer at Community Connect, Inc., the parent of Blackplanet.com (where she is a Managing Producer).

---

[57] Alexis Garrett Bowman Stodghill's natural father is (Harding) Reginald Bowman, Jr. (her mother's first husband, b. Dec. 26, 1952, in Philadelphia, Penn., elected to N.Y.C school board) the son of Harding Reginald Bowman (b. Apr. 4, 1921 in Orangeburg County, S.C.) and the former Phyllis Cluff (b. Sept. 18, 1930, in New York, New York). The parents of Harding Reginald Bowman were Ransom Bowman and the former Annie Jamison. Ransom Bowman's parents were Grant C. Bowman and the former Laura Kitt, who were also the parents of: Anna, Eliza, Pinkero, Mortimer, Rachel, Vanora, Josephine, Ollie, Grant, Jr., Judson, Malachi, and Ransom. A surviving deed establishes that Grant C. Bowman owned 334 acres of land in the town of Bowman, S.C. (Orangeburg County). The parents of Phyllis Cluff were Jesse Cluff and the former Rebecca Yeadon (b. Aug. 8, 1889; married on Dec. 26, 1926). Rebecca Yeadon's parents were Henry Cornelius Yeadon (b. June 16, 1860 in Charleston, S.C., d. Nov 1952 in Brooklyn, N.Y.) and the former Josephine Martin (b. Apr. 1, 1860 in Heightstown, N.J., d. 1932 in Brooklyn, N.Y.); they were also the parents of: Irene (White) Ellen Marie (Williams) Josephine, Henry C., Jr., George Henry, and Benjamin Oscar; Josephine Martin had a brother named Tom Martin whose children were Harrie and Tom, Jr.

The paternal ancestors of Alexis Garrett Bowman Stodghill:

Maternal grandmother, the former Phyllis Cluff, circa 1945 in Maine

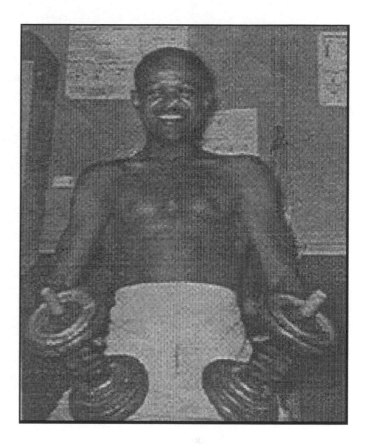

Paternal grandfather, Harding Bowman

Great-grandmother, Rebecca Yeadon Cluff

Rebecca's husband, Jesse Cluff

Rebecca's parents (Henry Cornelius Yeadon and the
former Josephine Martin) and one of her brothers

EDITOR'S DESK

Fortune.com editor Chris Peacock (left) and his team, Alexis Stodghill, Caldwell Toll, Lee Sharp, and Gabrielle Solomon, use online exclusives to attract more than seven million page views a month.

Click on fortune.com

Thinking about changing jobs, or just looking for career advice? Need more sophisticated investing tools? Crave the latest Wall Street chatter? If these topics interest you, we've got a ton of exclusive information—including stuff you won't find in the pages of FORTUNE—waiting for you on the newly redesigned pages of our Web alter ego, fortune.com.

In addition to a lot of what's in the magazine, fortune.com is trying harder than ever to add value on the Web by concentrating on three subjects: investing, careers, and information technology. And it's working. Right now we're generating some seven million page views a month.

For investors, of course, we offer our most famous Web personality, Andy Serwer, and his wacky/wise daily Street Life column, a tamer excerpt of which appears in the magazine. Online, you have the option of talking back to him instantaneously. And we now offer a direct link to fortuneinvestor.com, a service featuring advanced investing tools, market data, and analysis.

Our Career Resource Center carries a Web-exclusive version of Ask Annie, our career advice column, plus a newly forged link with Career Mosaic, one of the Internet's largest and most sophisticated job-listing sites. This is all in addition to a wealth of self-diagnostic quizzes, company research links, and career-related content drawn from the pages of the magazine.

For those who just can't wait to get FORTUNE's tech coverage, you can access regular columns from tech heavy-hitters Stewart Alsop, Bill Gurley, and Dick Shaffer even before they're on the newsstand, plus all our cutting-edge coverage from Silicon Valley. We've been online now for more than three years, and this is our third major Web redesign. It's a fast-moving medium. Stay tuned.

John W. Huey Jr.

MANAGING EDITOR

*Michael LeTwan Suber, and
his grandfather, (Willie) Carold Garrett*

Michael A. Suber, son of **Willie Carold Garrett** and Mrs. Rosa L. Rice; married Tawana Goode (daughter of Vera Hunter) producing one son: Michael LeTwan.

Michael LeTwan Suber (b. May 4, 1984) son of **Michael Suber** and the former Tawana Goode.

Alma Summers (b. Sept. 9, 1916) daughter of Mable Yeargins and **Albert Elton Garrett, I**; married and widowed by Henry Summers; mother of four daughters: Mable Lee (Duncan) Allie (McDuffie); Juliet (Ware); and Mary Anne.

Mary Anne Summers (b. May 29, 1952) daughter of the former **Alma** Yeargins and Henry **Summers**; attended North Carolina A&T.

James ("Jimmy") Sullivan, Jr. (b. Feb. 11, 1968) son of the former **Vivian Neely** and James A. Sullivan; married; one child.

Vivian Sullivan (b. May 24, 1921) daughter of the former **Pearl Neely (see "Roland") and Shellie Donaldson Garrett**; married James A. Sullivan on Jan. 1, 1957;[58] one son: James; resides in Greer, S.C..

Mary Lee Garrett Thompson (b. June 17, 1923; TWIN to Wister Pinckney (Paul)) daughter of **Albert Elton Garrett, I and the former Mattie Neely**; married and divorced Arthur Thompson; resides in Hickory Tavern, S.C.. on land once owned by her grandfather, Wick Garrett. Indeed, Mary was instrumental in preserving Wick's land for future generations: She acquired land from cousins who might otherwise have transferred title outside the family and has, herself, transferred land to members of the younger generation.

***Edward Jordan Tucker, Jr.** ("Sonny") (b. Nov. 12, 1955, d. 1999) only son of the former **Mattie Elton Garrett** and Edward Jordan **Tucker,** Sr.; married and divorced.

---

[58] James A. Sullivan was the son of the Rev. R.B. Sullivan and Birdie E.

The daughters of Mattie Elton Garrett Tucker

Mattie Tucker

*Mattie Elton Tucker** (b. Nov. 5, 1920, d. Aug. 29, 1998); eldest child of **Albert Elton Garrett, I and the former Mattie Neely**; married Edward Jordan Tucker on March 15, 1947,[59] the father of her four children: Sharyn (McCalla, formerly, Martin); Twins: Evangeline (Price) and Madeline (Gamble); and Edward; she enlisted in the Armed Forces during W.W. II, and served as a Technical Sergeant in the only Black WAC battalion to serve overseas. She worked as a court stenographer for a short time, before beginning her life career as a N.Y.C Corrections Officer, from which she retired in 1976.

Josephine Simons Wade ("Jo") (b. 1916) eldest child of the former **Mattie Phyllis Garrett** and Alfred **Simons**; attended Miner Teachers College before obtaining degree from New York University — AKA; married George W. Wade (who taught at the Howard University dental school) the father of her daughter, Phyllis (Logan); retired after 47 years of teaching; now a docent at the Smithsonian institute; she is in possession of a Threewitts family bible dating back to 1857.

---

[59] Edward Jordan Tucker, Sr., was the son of Beatrice Tucker, who was the daughter of Susie Tucker.

Looking North
To a Better Life

Many D.C. Blacks Have Roots
In 'The Great Migration'

FROM THE WASHINGTON POST.
Feb. 16, 1987

Juliet Ware (b. Aug. 1, 1942) daughter of the former **Alma** Yeargins and Henry **Summers**; married John Henry Ware, the father of her three children: Tracey Denise, John Eric, and Jennifer Ann; graduated from SCSU; teaches in Greenville schools.

McKinnezy Ware (b. May 13, 1995) granddaughter of **Juliet Ware**.

Tracey Denise Ware (b. July 14, 1969) **daughter** of the former **Juliet Summers** and John Henry **Ware**.

Wanda Priscilla Washington (b. Feb. 26, 1962) the only daughter among the nine children of the former **Lnora Garrett** and Curtis **Grayson**; first marriage on June 7, 1986, to Kevin McNair of Brooklyn, N.Y.; second marriage to Barry Denny; third marriage to Rob Washington; three children: Ryan Grayson, Kevin McNair, and Shirona Denny; attended Livingstone College in North Carolina.

Natasha Nicole Watkins, daughter of the former **Tonya Shawn Harris** and Marshall **Watkins**.

Tonya Shawn Watkins, daughter of the former **Patricia Ann Latimer** and Clifford **Harris;** married Marshall Watkins, the father of Natasha Nicole.

Branden Marquis White (b. 1993) son of **Martha Dorinda White**.

Brittany Marie White (b. 1989) son of **Martha Dorinda White**.

Martha Dorinda White (b. November 11, 1957) daughter of the former **Dorothy Dakers** and John Wesley **Smith**; married Warren White and is the mother of Brittany and Branden.

*****Carrie Lee Williams** (b. June 17, 1897, Laurens, S.C.) daughter of **Samuel Garrett** and the former Hattie Hunter; married Hunter Nathaniel Williams,

(Cornelia) Elaine Walker, daughter of **C.D. Beasley** and the former Lucinda Sherman; graduated from Presbyterian College in Clinton, SC; married Frank Walker, the father of her three children; they reside in a suburb of Atlanta, Ga.

Mary Joe Walker, daughter of the former **Eunice** Garrett and Willie **Ramage;** married Lloyd Walker;[60] a school principal at Bera High School in Greenville, S.C.; the mother of two daughters

Jennifer Ann Ware (b. Oct. 9, 1978) daughter of the former **Juliet Summers** and John Henry **Ware**.

John Eric Ware (b. Sept. 22, 1973) son of the former **Juliet Summers** and John Henry **Ware**.

---

[60] Mary Joe's husband, Lloyd,, is the brother of Frank Walker, the husband of the former Cornelia Elaine Beasley (also listed under Garretts).

Carrie Lee Garrett Williams

the father of her daughters, Catherine (Stoddard); Ruth (Stoddard); and Ruby (Latimer).

Cavernetta Sharon Williams, daughter of **C.D. Beasley** and the former Lucinda Sherman; she married A.P. Williams, III, the father of her two children; they reside in Columbia, SC.

Nia Endesha Halima Williams, daughter of **Dr. Phyllis Nicholson, M.D.** and David Williams; attended Penn State before transferring to New York University.

Lois Williams, daughter of **Fletcher Garrett**; last known residence was in Washington, D.C..

Corie Yeargins, daughter of **William Yeargins** and Winnie.

*****Isaac Yeargins** (b. Jan. 22, 1955; TWIN to Isaiah; d. Sept. 20, 1993), son of **Talma Yeargins** and the former Corrie Brewster.

Isaiah Yeargins (b. Jan. 22, 1955; TWIN to Isaac) son of **Talma Yeargins** and the former Corrie Brewster.

Michael B. Yeargins, son of **Talma Yeargins** and the former Corrie Brewster.

Nicole Yeargins, daughter of **Julia Bonaparte.**

Selina Yeargins, daughter of **William Yeargins** and Winnie; a beautician.

Talma Yeargins, son of Mabel Yeargins and **Albert Elton Garrett, I**; married the former Corrie Brewster, the mother of his six children: William, Talma, Jr., Twins: Isaac (deceased) and Isaiah, Michael B., and one daughter, Julia Ann (Bonaparte); lives in Greenville, S.C..

William Yeargins, son of **Talma Yeargins** and the former Corrie Brewster; married Winnie, producing three children: William, Jr., Selina, and Corie.

William Yeargins, Jr., son of **William Yeargins** and Winnie.

Sandra Young ("Peaches") daughter of **Leroy Kennedy**.

Thomas Weldon Garrett, Sr., LaBrenda Garrett-Nelson & Talma Yeargins, with Rosalynd Garrett in the foreground

Bobbinetta Young (b. Mar. 29, 1956) daughter of **Bobby Fletcher Garrett** and the former Mamie Smith; graphic artist; graduated from Lander College in S.C.; married and divorced Cornell McCanty, Jr.; and in 2000, married B.F. Young; she has one son named Dominique Garrett.

Mildred Young is the daughter of **Willie Jackson Beasley** and the former Katie Annette Wilson; married David Young, the father of her daughter, Rita (Henderson); she and her husband are retired teachers.

ADDENDUM:

Dominique Garrett (b. Nov. 20, 1986) son of **Bobbinetta** Garrett **Young**.

Edward Mack, Jr.

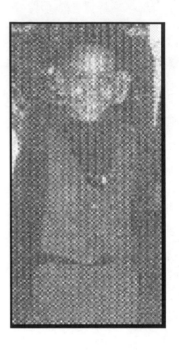

Dominique Garrett

Shelly Ruth Kimpson, Frances Bradley,
and Abigail Rogers Harris

Debra Jean Garrett and son, Tony

In Front are Thomas Weldon Garrett, Sr., Eddie Tucker, Sr., and Curtis Grayson
In back, from left, are Thomas's first wife, Eva, Leora Grayson, Mattie Tucker, Bobby Garrett and his first wife, Mamie, and Mary Garrett Thompson

THE NEELY FAMILY

"I will multiply thy seed as the stars of the heaven, and as the sand which is upon the sea shore; and thy seed shall possess the gate of his enemies."
Genesis, 22:17

Maria Hood

Maria-pronounced "Mariah"—Hood was the mother of Richard Neely.[61] Mattie Neely Garrett recalled that Maria Hood had a brother who was known as "Uncle Big Tom."

Richard Neely, Sr.

Richard Neely had two half brothers: Lee and Mack, who had a different surname because they grew up on a different plantation.[62] Richard Neely also had a half-brother named William Neely. Richard married the former Harriet Dial, fathering: William; John Pinckney; Richard, Jr.; Cora Estella; Walter; Mary (Neely); Berry Franklin; Lydie (Sullivan); and Corrie (Cleveland); he was also the father of Calvin Neely.

Relationship To The Garrett And Sullivan Families

Mattie Neely, a daughter of John Pinckney Neely and the former Missie Pinson, married Albert Elton Garrett, I, a son of Wick Garrett and the former Frances Latimer. Earlier, Richard Neely, Jr. married "Elp's" older sister, Beulah. Emma J. Irby, the maternal grandmother of Searight Sullivan's children by his second wife, Fannie, was the sister of the former Frances Latimer, and Maggie Sullivan, Searight Sullivan's sister, married Berry Franklin Neely, another son of Richard Neely, Sr. and the former Harriet Dial. Also, the former Etta Garlington, a grandchild of Haily Sullivan (and first cousin of Maggie and Searight Sullivan) married Walter Neely, a third son of Richard Neely Sr. and the former Harriet Dial. These legal relationships do not begin to tell the story of how close these families actually were. As noted above, Richard Neely, Jr. was among the first deacons at Bethel Hall church, and Neelys (such as O.T. and Robert Nesbitt) are still active members.

Hopewell Baptist Church

Hopewell, in the Ekom district of Laurens, was organized in 1869. Hopewell was the original home church of the Neelys. Wick Garrett and his family also attended Hopewell before Bethel Hall was founded. John Pinckney Neely's farm was situated

---

[61] Information regarding the Neely Family was compiled by LaBrenda Garrett-Nelson, daughter of Thomas Weldon Garrett, Sr., granddaughter of Mattie Neely Garrett, based, in part, on information obtained at the 1980 GNS reunion from Tony Grayson, Norma Y. Green, Cora Cleveland Mason, Arthuree Neely McCoy, and Inona McRae. In 1995, Linda Kumi obtained obituaries and photographs from her aunt, Ethel Price, providing a wealth of additional information.

[62] SOURCE: Mattie Neely Garrett.

near Hopewell, and he, his wife, and some of their children are buried there. (George) Quincy Neely served as the Superintendent of the Hopewell Sunday School for more than 50 years.

Richard Neely, Jr.

Richard Neely, Jr. (b. Aug. 16, 1882; d. Jan. 24, 1928) was a son of **Richard Neely, Sr.** and the former Harriet Dial; married the former **Beulah Garrett (see "Cleveland")** the mother of his ten children. Beulah was a daughter of Wick and Frances Garrett. Richard died an untimely death of pneumonia. The children of Richard and Beulah Neely are: Maude (Taylor); Mary Lee (Henderson); Celeste (Harris); Garrett; Houston; Ruth (Davenport); John Walter ("Jake"); Edgenora (Herron); Fonzel; and Homer.

Richard's children and grandchildren settled up and down the eastern seaboard of the United States, including Washington, D.C., New Jersey, and Connecticut. His granddaughter, Myrtle Taylor (a great-granddaughter of Wick Garrett) is a published poet. His son, Jake Neely (also a grandson of Wick Garrett) was a composer of popular songs. His great-grandson Lee Satterfield (a great-great-grandson of Wick Garrett) was appointed as a judge by then President of the United States, George Bush.

Walter Neely

Walter Neely was the son of **Richard Neely, Sr.** and the former Harriet Dial. He married the former **Etta Garlington** a granddaughter of Haily Sullivan (Listed under Sullivans). The couple had seven children: Corrie; Zettie; Debertie (Moore); Helen (Thompson); Alfonzo; Richard B.; and Smith.[63]

Walter Neely and his wife, the former Etta Garlington, with Corrie and Zetti

The Rev. Berry Franklin Neely

The Rev. Berry Franklin Neely was a son of **Richard Neely, Sr.** and the former Harriet Dial He was a building contractor and minister. In 1904, he married the former **Maggie Florence Sullivan,** a granddaughter of Haily Sullivan. Maggie was a dressmaker and designer. Berry and Maggie's eight children are: Celeste Terrell; Mary L. (Whinen); Ethel B. (Price); Hattie Bell (Pratt); Fosalee Maggie (Williams); Richard Perry; John Brooks; and Arthuree Alberta (McCoy). In 1916, Berry Franklin Neely moved his family to Sumter Country, S.C., where members of his immediate family still reside.

---

[63] From Alfonzo Neely's obituary

Berry & Maggie

From left: Ethel Price, Maggie Sullivan Neely, John Brooks Neely, Mozell Hopkins, Arthuree Neely McCoy, Willie Blanch Neely, M.L. Whinen, and Fosalee Williams

John Pinckney Neely

John Pinckney Neely (b. Dec. 25, 1871; d. Oct. 6, 1959) was a son of **Richard Neely, Sr.** and the former Harriet Dial. He married the former Missie Pinson (b. July 10, 1873; d. Aug. 25, 1953; the daughter of Peter and Pam Pinson.[64]) They had nine children: John Lee; Calvin; Elmer R.; Benjamin G.; Pearl L. (Roland); Willie Blanch; Inona (McRae); Mattie (Garrett); and Preston. He was also the father of George Quincy Neely. John Pinckney Neely was nearly as prosperous a farmer as Wick Garrett, the father-in-law of his daughter, Mattie, and his brother, Richard. His circumstances were reduced when he failed to sell before the bottom fell out of the cotton market during the Depression. Nevertheless, he was

---

[19]Peter and Pam Pinson were also the parents of Cora—who married Richard Bolt, producing four children: Glenn (d. Nov. 30, 1975) L.B., Buddy, and Lula (McCory) —Emma, and Twin Grant (who married Tessie Davenport, producing ten children: Lee Pinson (b. Nov. 25, 1909, who married Emma Griffin), Rosie (who married Lure Bell) Tessie (who married Vadray Kennedy) Azalee (who married Willie Irby) Beatrice (who married Joe W. Sweeney) Rhoena (who married Curtis Harding) Ellen Ruth (who married John Lovett) Lafayette (who married George McDaniel) Theodore, and Calvin) and Twin Grant, Lee. The Pinsons also hold family reunions that are attended by their Neely cousins.

The Jones Irby Family Reunion Program (1996) lists Willie Irby as the son of John Irby (the son of Margaret Irby) his siblings were John A., Corrie, Clara, Ezell, Irene, Theodore, Mary, Carrie Jessie, and Henry. From his marriage to Azalee Pinson, were children: Willie E., Dorothy Ruth, Josephs, and Devore

John & Missie Neely

able to leave to his children acreage in Pelzer, S.C., to which he moved from Laurens in the early 1940's.

Other descendants of Maria Hood, and Richard and Harriet Neely are:

Yohannon Alexander (b. Jan. 3, 1991) son of **Regina Neely** and her second husband, Dwight Alexander.

Jacqueline Anderson, daughter of **Leroy Sullivan** and the former Ethel Brown; married.

Aaron Blowe (b. Apr. 9, 1994) son of **the former Carol Neely** and Milton **Blowe**.

Carol Blowe (b. May 26, 1957) daughter of **Homer Neely** and Myrtle K.; married Milton Blowe, the father of her son, Aaron; she also has a stepson, Travis.

Anjanette D. Boyd (b. Feb. 19, 1966) is the daughter of the former **Johnnie Mae** Anderson and Willie Lee **Boyd,** the mother of two daughters: Laquisa Denise and Kiara Jane Hammary.

Aurelia Shantell Boyd (b. July 3, 1988) daughter of **Amelia Delaine Boyd Sheard.**

Johnnie Mae Boyd (b. Apr. 6, 1945, Laurens, S.C.) is the daughter of **Homer Neely** and Carrie Lee Anderson; she married (on Feb. 15, 1964) and divorced Willie Lee Boyd, and has three children: Anjanette D.; Amelia Delaine (Sheard) and Tammi; she resides in Laurens, S.C.

Laquisa Denise Boyd (June 30, 1987) daughter of **Anjanette D. Boyd.**

Tammi Michelle Boyd (b. May 11, 1971) is the daughter of the former **Johnnie Mae Anderson** and Willie Lee **Boyd.**

DeCarlos Bradley (b. Oct. 11, 1971) son of the former **Frances Alberta Neely** and George **Bradley**; attending the University of the District of Columbia, majoring in Business Administration, and employed by Tascom, Inc.

Crystal Bradley (b. July 24, 1969) daughter of the former **Frances Alberta Neely and** George **Bradley**; attending the University of the District of Columbia.

Frances Alberta Bradley, (b. June 23, 1934, Laurens, S.C.) daughter of the former **Maude Neely** (see "Taylor") and a Robinson married George Bradley, the father of her two children: DeCarlos and Crystal.

Brittani Brown (b. Aug. 31, 1983) daughter of **Larry Brown** and the former Delores Brockman.

Larry Brown (b. May 9, 1956) son of the former **Flora Sullivan** (now, **Harris**); married the former Delores Brockman, the mother of his children, Brittani and Mario.

Mario Brown (b. Dec. 16, 1986) son of **Larry Brown** and the former Delores Brockman.

Wallace Brown, son of the former **Flora Sullivan** (now, **Harris**).

Jessie Mae Byrd, daughter of the former **Lydie Neely** and Cade **Sullivan**; married Ezell Byrd (deceased) and they had two sons and two daughters.

Georgia Mae Carnely, daughter of **George Neely.**

Virginia Chapman, daughter of **Leroy Sullivan** and the former Ethel Brown; married.

*Clyde Cleveland (d. 1995) grandson of **Corrie Cleveland.**

*Corrie Cleveland, a daughter of **Richard Neely** and the former Harriet Dial; married James Cleveland; they had four children: Theodore, Irene (Johns) Rudolph, and Cora (Mason). Corrie was the grandmother of 12, the great-grandmother of 22, and the great-great-grandmother of five.

Corrie Neely Cleveland

Eddie Cleveland (b. 1962) son of **Rudolph Cleveland.**

*Rudolph Cleveland, son of the former **Corrie Neely** and James **Cleveland**, one son: Eddie.

*Theodore Cleveland, son of the former **Corrie Neely** and James **Cleveland.**

Dorothy Clinksdale, daughter of the former Flora Sullivan (now, **Harris**); married Calvin Clinksdale.

Candace C. Culcleasure, the daughter of the former **Evetter Sullivan** and Fred **Culcleasure.**

Cherrie C. Culcleasure, the daughter of the former **Evetter Sullivan** and Fred **Culcleasure.**

Bessie Beulah Crosson (b. Aug. 27, 1937) daughter of the former **Edgenora Neely** and Furman **Herron**; married and divorced James Crosson; mother of

Kenneth, Garey, Veronica (Jordan) and Raymond; resides in Washington, D.C..

Garey Crosson (b. June 9, 1962) son of the former **Bessie Herron (see "Crosson") and** James Crosson; attended Morgan State; married the former Naomi Kinney.

Kenneth Crosson (b. Oct. 9, 1956) son of the former **Bessie Herron (see "Crosson")** and James Crosson; graduate of the University of the District of Columbia (UDC); Contract Monitor, Office of the Vice President, Administrative Services, UDC.

RaeShawn L. Crosson (b. Apr. 1, 1982) daughter of **Raymond Crosson** and the former Barbara Gamble; will enter Temple University in the fall of 2000.

Raymond Crosson (b. Mar. 16, 1959) son of the former **Bessie Herron (see "Crosson")** and James Crosson; married the former Barbara Gamble on July 16, 1979; they have three children: Raymond Jr., RaeShawn L. and Shaun.

Raymond Crosson, Jr., son of **Raymond Crosson** and the former Barbara Gamble.

Shaun Crosson (b. Jan. 4, 1995) son of **Raymond Crosson** and the former Barbara Gamble.

Evetter Culcleasure, the daughter of **Leroy Sullivan** and the former Ethel Brown; married Fred Culcleasure.

Brittaine Chadell Cumby, daughter of **Rodney Neely**.

Shirley Cummings, daughter of **Alfonzo Neely** and the former Beatrice LaBoon.

Zipporah Daniels (b. Nov. 25, 1985) daughter of **Regina Neely**.

Holly Davenport, daughter of the former **Pamela Neely** and Randall **Davenport**.

Pamela Davenport, daughter of **Dee Ethel Neely**; married Randall Davenport, the father of daughter, Holly.

Ruth Davenport daughter of **Richard Neely, Jr. and the former Beulah Cora Garrett** (see "Cleveland"); married Sam Davenport.

Belinda Dukes (b. July 19, 1953) daughter of the former **Celeste Neely** and Edward **Harris;** married Albert Dukes (b. Mar. 1, 1943) the father of her two children: Durell and Celese; also raised three stepchildren: Francis, Jacqueline, and Leon.

Celese Dukes, daughter of the former **Belinda Harris** and Albert **Dukes**.

Durell Dukes (b. Dec. 22, 1984) son of the former **Belinda Harris** and Albert **Dukes**.

Bennie (Mae) Durden, daughter of **Benjamin Neely** and the former Willie Mae Coleman; married Russell Durden, the father of her daughter, Desiree.

Desiree Durden, daughter of the former **Bennie Neely** and Russell **Durden**.

James Eichelberger, son of **Jim Eichelberger**. He identified his mother as A "Hood" who was a sister to John Pinckney Neely's mother, and was called cousin by John Pinckney Neely and others (as reported by Robert Nesbitt Neely).

Jean Franklin, daughter of the former **Sue Pearl Neely** and Mr. **Franklin**.

Kenneth Franklin, son of **the former Sue Pearl Neely** and Mr. **Franklin**.

Sue Pearl Franklin, daughter of the former **Mary Neely** and John R. **Neely;** mother of Mary Anne (Gadson) Kenneth, and Jean.

Desmond Gadson, son of the former **Mary Anne** Franklin and Robert **Gadson;** attended Tuskegee and University of South Florida.

*Nicky & Mary Anne Gadson
at the 1983 GNS Reunion*

Mary Anne Gadson, daughter of the former **Sue Pearl Neely** and Mr. **Franklin**; married Robert Gadson; three children: Nicole, Robert, and Desmond; resides in Tampa, Florida.

Nicole ("Nicky") Gadson, daughter of the former **Mary Anne** Franklin and Robert **Gadson;** graduated from Florida A & M.; the mother of a son.

Robert Gadson, son of the former **Mary Anne** Franklin and Robert **Gadson;** graduated from Florida A & M; an electrical engineer.

*Mattie Neely Garrett with five of her
great-grandchildren: Craig Garrett,
Michelle Martin, Alexis Garrett Stodghill (in lap),
Nicole Price, and Teresa Garrett*

Mattie Neely Garrett (b. Mar. 17, 1898, Laurens, S.C.; d. Nov. 30, 1986) daughter of **John Pinckney Neely** and the former Missie Pinson; was a teacher before marriage to Albert Elton Garrett, I on Dec. 28, 1919 (see his entry for the names of their eleven children).

Chester Gibson, son of **Lydia Gibson.**

Norma Green, daughter of the former **Ollie Neely** and Booker T. **Yarbrough**; married Samas L. Green.

Shelby Ananie Goodwin (b. Laurens, S.C.) daughter of **O.T. Neely** and the former Mary Dial; graduated from Winthrop College with a degree in psychology and obtained a masters in social work from the

University of South Carolina; she is an adoption specialist; married Calvin Leon Goodwin, a lawyer who graduated from Lander University and obtained his law degree from Southern University School of Law; now resident in Columbia, S.C..

Kiara Jane Hammary (b. Mar. 6, 1990) daughter of **Anjanette D. Boyd**.

Celeste Harris (b. Nov. 16, 1925, Laurens, S.C.) daughter of **Richard Neely, Jr. and the former Beulah Cora Garrett (see "Cleveland")**; married Edward Harris, the father of her three children: Larry; Phyllis (Jacobs); and Belinda (Dukes); resident of New Jersey.

Chanel Harris, daughter of **Wanda Harris**.

Flora (formerly, Brown) Harris, daughter of the former **Lydie Neely** and Cade **Sullivan**; married the Reverend Clifton Harris on Feb. 21, 1986; the mother of two sons, Larry and Wallace, and two daughters, Lydia (Sweeney) and Dorothy (Clinksdale); resident of Greenville, S.C.

Jamal Harris (b. Apr. 2, 1979), son of **Larry Harris** and the former Grace King.

Kalana Harris (b. July 10, 1978) daughter of **Larry Harris** and the former Grace King.

Larry Harris, son of the former **Celeste Neely** and Edward **Harris**; married the former Grace King; they had two children: Jamal and Kalana.

Travis Harris, son of **Wanda Harris**.

Wanda Harris, daughter of **Quincy Neely**; married and the mother of Chanel and Travis.

*****Mary Lee Henderson** (b. Jan. 18, 1923, Laurens, S.C.; d. Oct. 14, 1973) daughter of **Richard Neely, Jr. and the former Beulah Garrett (see "Cleveland:)**; married Chester Henderson, the father of her two children: Lydia (Gibson) and Otis.[65]

Otis Henderson ("Brother"), son of the former **Mary Lee Neely** and Chester **Henderson**.

---

[65] From Mary Lee Henderson's obituary

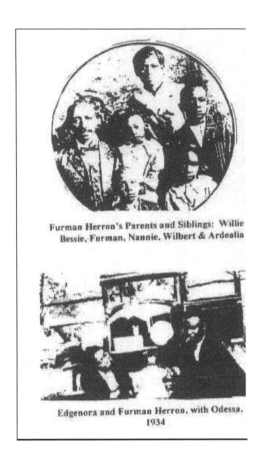

Furman Herron's Parents and Siblings: Willie
Bessie, Furman, Nannie, Wilbert & Ardealia

Edgenora and Furman Herron, with Odessa,
1934

*Edgenora Herron (b. Laurens, S.C.; d. 1980) daughter of the former Beulah Garrett (see "Cleveland") and Richard Neely, Jr.; married Furman Herron, the father of her two children: Lorena (Satterfield) and Bessie (Crosson); their oldest child, Odessa, died in infancy.[66]

---

[66] Furman Herron (b. 1906; d. 1995) was the son of Willie and Bessie Herron of Gray Court, S.C.. Willie and Bessie were also the parents of Nannie, who married Alonzo Bates-the father of Willie James and Anne Harriet; Wilbert, who married the former **Minnie Bell Hunter**-the mother of Willie Belton, Parthenia (Mosley) Alma (Carr) and Elizabeth (Grice); and Ardealia, who married William Russell Hill- the father of Novella (Nesbitt). Willie Herron was the son of Richmond and Delia Herron, who came from the Dial plantation and settled in Gray Court. Richmond and Delia were also the parents of Holly, Katie, Mattie, and Minnie. **Minnie Bell Herron** was the daughter of Belton Hunter, a son of Alfred Hunter (see "Hunters" in the Table of Contents); her daughters included her photograph in the Flat Ruff 120th anniversary program.

1976: Edgenora and Furman Herron, surrounded by daughter (Bessie Crosson (to their left), Lorena Satterfield (to their right), Lorena's husband, Lee, Sr., and Lorena and Lee's daughter, Lori. Standing (from left): Kenneth Crosson, Garey Crosson, Lawrence Satterfield, Bessie's daughter, Veronica, Raymond Crosson, and Lee Furman Satterfield.

John Hill and Meredith C. Hill, descendant of **Calvin & Ollie Neely.**

Anthony Hood, son **of Calvin** Hood and Vivian.

Calvin Hood, son of the former **Hattie Lula Neely** and David **Hood**; married Vivian; two sons: Anthony and Darryl; resides in Cleveland, Ohio.

Carla Hood, daughter of **Edward Hood** and the former Joyce Davis.

Darryl Hood, son of **Calvin Hood.**

***Donald Hood,** son of the former **Hattie Lula Neely** and David **Hood,** married the former Sally Smith; they had two children: Donald, Jr. and Ronald.

Donald Hood, Jr., son of **Donald Hood** and the former Sally Smith.

Edward Hood, son of the former **Hattie Lula Neely** and David **Hood**; married the former Joyce Davis, the mother of his child, Carla.

(Hattie) Lula Hood, daughter of **Calvin Neely** and the former Ollie Cleveland; married David Hood, the father of her three children: Donald, Calvin, and Edward.

***Mozel Hopkins** (b. July 1, 1924; d. Nov. 26, 1971) daughter of the former **Pearl Neely** and George E. **Roland**; married William Hopkins, Jr.

Danielle Jacobs, daughter of the former **Phyllis Harris** and Edward **Jacobs**.

Phyllis Jacobs (b. Aug. 8, 1950) daughter of the former **Celeste Neely** and Edward **Harris**; married with one child named Danielle.

Alan Jeter, son of **James Jeter** and Marian.

***Beonia Jeter** (b. Sept. 7, 1907, Laurens, S.C.; d. Apr. 22, 1988) daughter of John R. Neely and the former **Mary Neely;** married Major James Jeter, the father of her three children: Beonia Pearl, Thelma Lee, and (Major) James.

Jordan Jeter, son of **Glenn J. Jeter** and the former Donna Bergeron.

Glenn J. Jeter son of **James Jeter**, married the former Donna Bergeron[67] on May 24, 1986; they had a daughter named Morgan and a son named Jordan; Glenn graduated from Seton Hall.

***(Major) James Jeter** (d. 1997), son of the former **Beonia Neely** and Major **Jeter**, married Marian, the mother of his three sons: Kurt, Glenn, and Alan.

Kurt Jeter, son of **James Jeter** and Marian.

Morgan Jeter, daughter of **Glenn J. Jeter** and the former Donna Bergeron.

Thelma Lee Jeter daughter of the former **Beonia Neely** and Major **Jeter**.

Cleophus Johns, Jr. (b. 1962) son of the former **Irene Cleveland** and Cleophus **Johns**.

***Irene Johns** (d. February 1974) daughter of the former **Corrie Neely** and James **Cleveland**; married Cleophus Johns, the father of her only child, Cleophus Johns, Jr.

Dierdre Elaine Townsend Johnson (b. June 23, 1962) daughter of the former **Lillian Maude** Fuller and Wade **Townsend**; married Maurice Johnson, the father of her two sons, Quincy and Wesley; graduated from Livingston College at Rutgers University.

Quincy Johnson (b. Nov. 24, 1992) son of the former **Dierdre Elaine Townsend** and Maurice **Johnson**.

Wesley Johnson (b. Jan. 18, 1993) son of the former **Dierdre Elaine Townsend** and Maurice **Johnson**.

Barbara Neely Jones, daughter of **George Neely**.

Veronica Jordan (b. Mar. 28, 1961) daughter of the former **Bessie Herron** (see "Crosson") and James Crosson; married Robert Jordan; attended Howard University.

Akousa Korantema Kumi (b. Jan. 11, 1976) daughter of the former **Linda Bonita McCoy** and Kwami Kumi; attended Montgomery College and Barber-Scotia College; currently attends Bowie State University, majoring in biology.

---

[67] Donna Bergeron was the daughter of Mr. and Mrs. Melvin Bergeron of Houston, Texas.

Elijah and his mother (1999)

Cora Mason, Quincy Neely, & Mrs. Benjamin Neely (Willie Mae) at Bethel Hall in 1986

Elijah Anthony Kwasi Kumi (b. Dec. 6, 1998), son of **Akousa Korantema Kumi.**

Linda Bonita Kumi (**"Bonnie"**) (b. Apr. 1, 1947) daughter of the former **Arthuree Neely** and Raleigh W. McCoy, married Kwami Kumi (a native of Ghana) the father of her two children: Akousa Korantema Ree Kumi and Kwabena Debiate Lee Kumi; graduated from Adelphi University in 1968, Garden City, N.Y.; also received a B.S. in information systems management, University of Maryland; and a masters in African studies from Howard University; resides in Silver Spring, Md.

*Linda Bonita Kumi and husband, Kwami,
on their wedding day*

Kwabena Debiate Lee Kumi (b. Sept. 13, 1977) son of the former **Linda Bonita McCoy** and Kwami **Kumi;** attends Lincoln University; graduated from the University of Illinois at Urbana-Champagne in 2000, with a bachelor of science in computer science from the School of Engineering.

Bennie Lattermore, granddaughter of **Jim Eichelberger** by his daughter.

Nayla J. Lackhart (b. Aug. 17, 1976), granddaughter of **Cora Mason**.

Lou Lewers, daughter of **Leroy Sullivan** and the former Ethel Brown; married James Lewers, the father of Jinsine, Linfred, Aaron, Edwin, and Jemika.

Sandra Neely Long (listed in the obituary of **Murray Neely** as his niece; last known residence in 1987 was Charleston, S.C.).

Calvin Mason, son of the former **Cora Cleveland** and Erman J. **Mason.**

Cora Mason (b. May 31, 1926) daughter of the former **Corrie Neely** and James **Cleveland;** married Erman J. Mason (d. May 12, 1986); they had six children: Rudolph, Calvin, Denise, Erma Jean, Lorlashone, and Thomas; was employed at McClellan Air Force Base for 27 years; she has a granddaughter named Nayla who was born in 1976.

Denise Mason, daughter of the former **Cora** Cleveland and Erman J. **Mason**; attended Sacramento City College.

Erma Jean Mason (b. Apr. 21, 1961) daughter of the former **Cora** Cleveland and Erman J. **Mason**; attended Sacramento State University while working at the city of Sacramento Police department.

Lorlashone Mason, daughter of the former **Cora** Cleveland and Erman J. **Mason**.

Rudolph Mason, son of the former **Cora** Cleveland and Erman J. **Mason**, one daughter..

Linda McCoy Kumi, with husband, Kwame, son, Kwabena, and daughter, Akousa

Thomas Mason, son of the former **Cora** Cleveland and Erman J. **Mason**.

*__Inona McRae__ (b. Jan. 22, 1905; Laurens, S.C.; d. December 1992) daughter of **John Pinckney Neely** and the former Missie Pinson; married Osie McRae; obtained a B.S. in education from Morris College in Sumter, S.C., where she taught for five years before moving to New York.

Allison Rooney McCoy, (b. Dec. 20, 1982) daughter of **Raymond Allan McCoy** and the former Clara Rooney.

Arthur Ray McCoy, (b. June 22, 1967) son of **Raymond Allan McCoy** and the former Clara Rooney.

Mark Allan McCoy

Arthur Ray McCoy

Raleigh and Arthuree McCoy

Allison McCoy (1992)

*Arthuree Alberta McCoy ("Ree") (b. Oct. 7, 1922, d. April 3, 1988) daughter of the Rev. **Berry Franklin Neely** and the former **Maggie Sullivan**; graduated from Morris College in South Carolina, also did graduate work at Bank Street College in New York, and Hunter College, City University; married Raleigh W. McCoy, the father of her two children: Raymond Allan and Linda Bonita (Kumi). Arthuree and her daughter contributed to a published collection of essays entitled "Tapping Potential: English and Language Arts For the Black Learner," published by the National Council of Teachers of English (1985) edited by Charlotte K. Brooks. Both she and her husband were N.Y.C. teachers. Arthuree spearheaded the revival of our family reunions, beginning with the 1980 session.

Erina Margaret McCoy (b. Feb. 19, 1977) daughter of **Raymond Allan McCoy** and the former Clara Rooney. Erina graduated from Sanoma State University in 1999, with a degree in communication. She immediately went to work as an assistant to Dr. Dean Adell, a medical Talk Show and TV answer-man for Channel 7 TV in San Francisco, and is now working as the weekend news anchorperson and a reporter for a TV station in Eureka, California.

Mark Allan McCoy (b. June 22, 1967) son of **Raymond Allan McCoy** and the former Yvonne Johnson.

Raymond Allan McCoy (b. June 5, 1944) son of the former **Arthuree Neely** and Raleigh W. **McCoy**; married the former Clara Rooney, a native of Ireland, the mother of three of his children: Erina Margaret, Allison, and Arthur Ray (who was named after his paternal grandmother and his father); graduated in 1990 from National University in Sacramento, with a degree in business and computer applications; has one son from first marriage to the former Yvonne Johnson: Mark Allan McCoy; retired as T/.Sgt. from U.S. Air Force after 22 years; resides in California.

Raymond Allan McCoy

Lorraine McDonald, daughter of **Leroy Sullivan** and the former Ethel Brown; married.

Karlos Mills, [son of **Dee Ethel Neely**, married Carolyn Smith, producing Malika.?]

Ethel Montgomery, daughter of the former **Ollie Neely** and Booker T. **Yarbrough**; married Jerry Montgomery, the father of Jerry Jr.

Jerry Montgomery, Jr., son of the former **Ethel Yarbrough** and Jerry **Montgomery**.

Aaron Ellington Moore, the son of Dr. **Gerian Steven Moore** and Nancy L.

***Debertie Moore**, daughter of **Walter Neely and the former Etta Garlington**; married Gerian Marshall Moore, the father of her two sons: Ellington Cortez Moore (deceased) and Gerian Steven Moore.

***Dr. Ellington Cortez Moore** (Ed. D.) (b. Dec. 9, 1932; d. June 10, 1992) son of the former **Debertie Neely** and Gerian Marshall **Moore**; he received his B.S. and M.S. from South Carolina State College, and an Ed. D. from the University of Massachusetts; after working for eight years in the public school system of Orangeburg, S.C., he served the State Department of Education for 21 years; he married Vashti G..

Dr. Gerian Steven Moore, son of the former **Debertie Neely** and Gerian Marshall **Moore**; he married Nancy L.; his sons are Solomon A., Joshua D., and Aaron Ellington.

Joshua D. Moore, the son of Dr. **Gerian Steven Moore** and Nancy L.

Solomon A. Moore, the son of Dr. **Gerian Steven Moore** and Nancy L..

Avieante Kotera Neely ("Teri") (b. Mar. 9, 1986) daughter of **Stanley Neely** and the former Sharon Evans.

Avieante Kotera Neely

Alfonzo Neely son of **Walter Neely** and the former **Etta Garlington**; married the former Beatrice LaBoon; five children: Shirley (Cummings) Joyce (Sullivan) Linda Gail (Parker) Jerry and Jerome.

Ben Neely, son of **E.C.** and Lonnie **Neely**; married Nancy; one child: Betty Ann.

Benjamin Neely (b. Jan. 11, 1916, Laurens, S.C.) youngest son of **John Pinckney Neely** and the former Missie Pinson; married the former Willie Mae Coleman, the mother of his daughter, Bennie Mae (Durden). Benjamin and Willie Mae celebrated their 50th Wedding anniversary at a formal reception in Ridgewood, N.Y. on Oct 15, 1987; resides in Brooklyn, N.Y.. He is a deacon at the Concord Baptist Church in Brooklyn, N.Y., where the renowned Reverend Doctor Gardner Taylor was pastor for many years; many of his Garrett nieces and nephews and their children living in New York joined him at this church.

Bonita Neely, daughter of **Mitchell Neely, Jr.** and Lula.

Betty Ann Neely, daughter of **Ben Neely** and Nancy.

Brittanica Neely, daughter of **Rodney Neely** and the former Carolina Dennis.

***Calvin Neely**, son of **John Pinckney Neely** and the former Missie Pinson; married Louise.

***Calvin Neely**, son of **Richard Neely, Sr.**; married the former Ollie Cleveland, the mother of his five children: Richard, Hattie Lula (Hood) Ollie (Yarbrough) Mitchell, Frances, and Dee Ethel.

***Celeste Terrell Neely** was the daughter of **Berry Franklin Neely and the former Maggie Florence Sullivan; she died as a teenager.**

1982: Standing: Curtis and Lnora Grayson, Bennie Durden, Elp Garrett, II, and Paul and Leanease Garrett. Seated are Inona McRae, Willie Mae and Benjamin Neely, Mrs. Elmer Neely (Katie), and Kimberly Garrett

Cora Estella Neely (b. Laurens, S.C.; d. Jan. 7, 1977) daughter of **Richard Neely** and the former Harriet Dial; she received her B.S. degree from Morris College in Sumter, S.C., and taught in the Laurens and Greenville County schools for 40 years.

Cora Estella Neely

Danielle Elizabeth Neely, daughter of Rodney Neely and the former Carolina Dennis.

Danny Neely, son of **Richard Neely** and the former Ruth Horton; father of one child.

Dee Ethel Neely, daughter of **Calvin Neely** and the former Ollie Cleveland; mother of John Marshall, Pamela (Davenport) and Karlos Tyrone.

Donald Neely, son of **Richard Neely** and the former Ruth Horton.

E.C. Neely, son of John R. Neely; married Lonnie; father of Otis T., Ben, Furman, Willie C., and William Oscar (**see Mary Neely**).

Ellen M. Neely, daughter of **Robert Nesbitt** Neely and the former Mildred Barksdale; a college graduate.

*Elmer Neely (deceased) son of **John Pinckney Neely** and the former Missie Pinson; married Katie, the mother of his daughter, Regina (once called Sauoda); lived in Brooklyn, N.Y..

Funtella Rashid Neely, son of **Stanley Neely** and the former Sharon Evans.

*Fonzel Neely (b. Laurens, S.C.; d.) son of **Richard Neely, Jr. and the former Beulah Garrett (see "Cleveland")**; married Victoria (a sister of his brother Houston's wife, Willie Gene) fathering two children: Winzel and a daughter (who died at age sixteen from meningitis).

Frances Neely, daughter of the former Ollie Cleveland and **Calvin Neely.**

Furman Neely, son of **E.C. Neely** and Lonnie; married the former Carolyn Anetta Williams,[68] the mother of his sons, Rodney Lotharia and Stanley Funtello; he resides in Laurens, S.C..

Garrett Neely, son of **Richard Neely, Jr.** and the former **Beulah Cora Garrett (see "Cleveland").**

George Neely, son of John R. Neely (husband of the former **Mary Neely**).

Gershaun Neely, as reported by Edward Mack, Jr., His parents were **Jerry** and Gail **Neely**, and James Neely was his grandfather; he also has an aunt named Willie Mae. (It is unclear whether he is a son of the Jerry Neely listed below).

---

[68] Carolyn Williams was the daughter of Hunter Nathaniel Williams, and his second wife, the former Alma Hunter; thus, Carolyn is the half-sister of Nathaniel's children by his first wife, the former Carrie Lee Garrett (listed above under "Garretts").
SOURCE: Lillie Williams-Tim, Carolyn's sister.

Homer Neely (b. Laurens, S.C., d. 1997) son of **Richard Neely, Jr.** and the former **Beulah Garrett** (see "Cleveland"); married Myrtle K., the mother of his three children: Jerome, Marvin, and Carol (Blowe); also the father of Johnnie Mae (Anderson) Boyd.

*****Houston Neely** (b. Laurens, S.C.; d.) son of **Richard' Neely, Jr. and the former Beulah Garrett** (see "Cleveland"); married Willie Gene (a sister of his brother Fonzel Neely's wife, Victoria) one daughter: Sherry (deceased, she married and had one daughter); also the father of Lillian Maude Townsend; lived in New Jersey.

Houston and Gene Neely

Jerome Neely, son of **Alfonzo Neely** and the former Beatrice LaBoon.

Jerome Malcome Neely (b. Aug. 31, 1952) son of **Homer Neely** and Myrtle K. Neely; married the former Deborah Ray, the mother of his son, Trevor.

Jerry Neely, son of **Alfonzo Neely** and the former Beatrice LaBoon.

John Neely, son of **E.C** and Lonnie **Neely.**

John Brooks Neely, son **of the Rev. Berry Franklin Neely** and the former **Maggie Sullivan.**

John Lee Neely (b. Mar. 6, 1903, Laurens, S.C.; d. June 10, 1966) son of **John Pinckney Neely** and the former Missie Pinson; married the former Georgia Mae Smith.

John R. Neely, his mother was a first cousin to sisters, Harriet Dial and the mother of Jim Eichelberger as reported by Robert Nesbitt Neely, per Jim Eichelberger. The first edition of this book erroneously indicated that he was not a blood relative. John R. Neely was the son of Henry Neely; Henry Neely was also the father of a daughter, Early, and three other sons: Samuel, John, and Joseph. John R. Neely's children (and Mary Neely's stepchildren) by a previous marriage were Twin daughters: M.L. and Inell (Makins); Clayton H.; Robert Nesbitt; George and Margie. E.C. and daughter, Roberta, were born to John Neely and a subsequent wife (reported by Thomas Weldon Garrett, Sr.). His other children are listed under Mary Neely's entry.

***John Walter Neely** ("Jake") son of **Richard Neely** and the former **Beulah Garrett (see "Cleveland")**; he married Clara, and was the father of two daughters, Melody and Crystal; he also raised his step-son, Tyrone; he was a composer of musician; Bessie Crosson (listed under Neelys) provided an original copy of the sheet music for one of his published songs:

Sheet music for one of John Walter Neely's songs (Nordyke Publishing Company, copyright July 11, 1948)

Kishana Leah Neely (b. Mar. 1, 1974) daughter of **Richard Juan Neely** and the former Ethel Jackson.

M.L. Neely, daughter of John R. Neely (husband of **Mary Neely**); mother of Cora Altamease (Lyons).

Bessie Crosson, M. L. Neely, and C.D. Beasley

Marvin Neely (b. Dec. 10, 1950) son of **Homer Neely** and Myrtle K.

*****Mary Neely**, daughter of **Richard Neely, Sr.** and the former Harriet Dial; married John R. Neely (a second cousin on her mother's side)[69] the father of her six children: Earlye; John Earl; Sue Pearl (Franklin); Hattie; Beonia (Jeter); and Prince.

Mitchell Neely, son of **Calvin Neely** and the former Ollie Cleveland; married the former Luida Davis, the mother of Mitchell, Jr.

Mitchell Neely, Jr., son of **Mitchell Neely** and the former Luida Davis; married Lula, the mother of his two daughters: Bonita, and Sandretta; resides in Detroit, MI.

*****Murray Lee Neely** (b. Feb. 28, 1917, Laurens, S.C.; d. Aug. 18, 1987) son of **William Neely** and the former Essie Shaw; he married the former Elnora Odessa Speed; he earned a B.S.. from Florida A & M and an Masters. from Ohio State University; he was named to the Florida A&M Sports Hall of Fame as a student athlete in 1978; his lifelong career was in the fields of coaching and education: he arrived at North Carolina A&T in 1950, where he coached football and track, and became known as "The Rock." He retired from NCA&T in 1978, and was inducted into the NCA&T State University Sports Hall of Fame in 1986.

Nesbitt Ezell Neely, son of **Robert Nesbitt Neely** and the former Mildred Barksdale.

Otis T. Neely, son of **E.C.** and Lonie **Neely**; married Mary; four children: Shelby (Goodwin); Debra (Tolbert); and two sons each of whom have the initials O.T.: Otis Thomas.

*****(George) Quincy Neely** (b. July 22, 1895; d. Feb. 2, 1988) son of **John Pinckney Neely** and the former Nellie Durham; married the former Mary Jane Todd; served in the U.S. Army as a private during WW I; father of Ella Mae.[70]

---

69 The Rev. Samuel B. Neely was a speaker at New Prospect Missionary Baptist Church's Sept. 17, 1994 anniversary banquet for Rev. Norman P. Pearson (the pastor of Bethel Hall in Hickory Tavern); he identified himself to LaBrenda Garrett-Nelson as a relative of O.T. Neely and a grandson of Samuel Neely

70 SOURCE: Obituary of George Quincy Neely.

Regina Neely (b. Nov. 5, 1952) daughter **of Elmer Neely** and Katie; married first to Elmino Thomas, the father of daughter, Rema Thomas; second marriage to Dwight Alexander, the father of son, Yohannon Alexander; also the mother of daughter, Zipporah Daniels; resident in Philadelphia, Penn.

Richard Neely, son of **Calvin Neely** and the former Ollie Cleveland; married the former Ruth Horton, the mother of his four children: Donald, Diane, Emma Jean, and Danny.

Richard B. Neely, son of the former **Etta Garlington and Walter Neely**.

Richard Eric Neely (b. May 24, 1970) son of **Richard Juan Neely** and the former Ethel Jackson.

Regina Neely & daughter, Zipporah

Richard Juan Neely

Richard Perry Neely, his wife, Henrietta, and son, Richard Juan

*Richard Juan Neely (b. May 29, 1942; d. Feb. 6, 1992) son of Richard Perry Neely and the former Henrietta Chisom; married (on Aug. 17, 1966) the former Ethel Jackson),[71] the mother of his two children: Richard Erik and Kishana Leah; he attended City College, City University of New York. [72]

Richard Perry Neely (d. 1943) son of the Rev. Berry Franklin Neely and the former Maggie Sullivan; married the former Henrietta Chisom, the mother of his son, Richard Juan Neely.

Robert Nesbitt Neely, (b. Nov. 4, 1925) son of John R. Neely (see Mary Neely); married Mildred Barksdale,[73] the mother of his daughter, Ellen M. and son, Nesbitt Ezell.

Rodney Latharia Neely, son of Furman Neely and the former Carolyn Williams; married the former Carolina Dennis, the mother of his daughter, Danielle Elizabeth; he is also the father of Brittaine Chadell Cumby. Rodney worked for the Greenville County Police for four years, as a police office and a detective; he now runs a security service.

---

[71] Ethel Jackson was born in Benton Mississippi, the child of McKinley Jackson and Willie Mae Mitchell.

[72] After the death of Richard Juan's father in 1943, his mother married Leon P. Sealey, their children (and Richard Juan's half-sister and brother) were Gloria Leona (Sealey) Whitaker and Leon P. Sealey, Jr.

[73] Mildred Barksdale (Sept. 28, 1924 – May 29, 1990) was a member of the same family as the wife of Shellie Donaldson Garrett (Alberta Barksdale) and the husband of the former Katherine Beasley (Dial Barksdale).

Rodney L. Neely provided security when Miss America 1994, Kimberly Aikens, visited Laurens

Willie Blanch Neely

Sandretta Neely, the daughter of **Mitchell Neely, Jr.** and Lula.

Smith W. Neely (b. Nov. 21, 1915, Laurens, S.C.; d. 1991) son of **Walter Neely** and the former **Etta Garlington**; served in the U.S. Army during WW II and was a retiree of J.P. Stevens; married the former Leola Gladden,[74] the mother of his daughter, Sandra Lee (Smith).

Stanley Funtella Neely, son of the former Carolyn Williams and **Furman Neely**; married the former Sharon Evans,[75] the mother of his daughter, Avieante Kotera, and son, Funtella Rashid; resides in Laurens, S.C..

Trevor Neely (b. Apr. 29, 1987) son of **Jerome Malcome Neely** and the former Deborah Ray.

*****Willie Blanch Neely** (b. Nov. 25, 1900, Laurens, S.C.; d. June 13, 1985) daughter of **John Pinckney Neely** and the former Missie Pinson; graduated from Morris College in Sumter, S.C., and taught school in Laurens and Greenville Counties for 44 years.

*****Willie C. Neely** (d. June 16, 1999) son of **E.C. Neely** and Lonnie; married the former Magnolia Peaks.

Willie H. Neely (b. Sept. 2, 1913; d. Oct. 28, 1983) married Lonice (he is listed as a brother in Earlye Rogers' obituary).

---

[74] Leola was the daughter of Henry Gladden of Chester, SC.
[75] Sharon is the daughter of Vera and Luther Evans.

William Neely

Hattie Bell Pratt

*Willie James Neely, son of the former Ollie Cleveland and **Calvin Neely**.

*William Neely son of **Richard Neely, Sr.** and the former Harriet Dial; married the former Essie Shaw, the mother of his son, Murray.

Winzel Neely, the son of **Fonzel Neely** and Victoria.

William Oscar Neely, son of **E.C. Neely** and Lonnie.

Linda Gail Parker, daughter of **Alfonzo Neely** and the former Beatrice Laboon.

Hattie Bell Pratt (b. July 22, 1910, d. Aug. 3, 1999, in an automobile accident) daughter of **the Rev. Berry Franklin and the former Maggie Sullivan**; married Milton Pratt; a dressmaker and designer (as her mother was).

Hattie as a young woman

from Left, Willie Blanch Neely, Ethel Price, Vivian Sullivan, and Cora Estella Neely

Ethel B. Price, daughter of **the Rev. Berry Franklin Neely and the former Maggie Florence Sullivan;** she was an educator who married John Ollie. Price;[76] one son: James Oliver Price (deceased).

James Oliver Price, Jr., son of **James Oliver Price** and the former Veronica Singleton; married in June 1996.

*James Oliver Price, Sr. (b. Oct 22, 1950; d. Jan. 22, 1980) son of the former **Ethel B. Neely**; and John Ollie. **Price** married the former Veronica Singleton, mother of his son, James, Jr. and a daughter, Tanya.

---

[76] John Ollie Price was born on Nov. 15, 1908, the son of William Price and the former Clattie Edwards, who were also the parents of Bertha (Alston) and three other sons: June, Dewey, and Roy.

James Oliver Price, Jr.

James Oliver Price, Sr.

*Earlye Rogers and her first cousin, once removed,
Mary Garrett Thompson*

Tanya Price, daughter of **James Oliver Price, Sr.**
and the former Veronica Singleton.

***Earlye Rogers** (b. Oct. 28, 1900, Laurens, S.C.; d.
Nov. 25, 1982) daughter of the former **Mary Neely**
and John R. Neely; married, adopted son is Roy Lee
Rogers.

*Ina Roland with her paternal grandmother's brother,
Benjamin Neely, and his first cousin, Hattie Pratt*

Lydia Gibson Riddick ("**Lottie**") daughter of the
former **Mary Lee Neely** and Chester **Henderson**;
married and the mother of four: Chester.

Lottie Riddick

George Roland son of the former **Pearl Neely** and George **Roland**; married the former Frankie Craig, the mother of his two children: George Anthony ("Tony") and (Stephanie) Ina; George (a retired teacher) Frankie (a pharmacist) and both of their children graduated from Texas Southern University

George Anthony Roland ("Tony") son of **George Roland** and the former Frankie Craig; graduate of Texas Southern University.

(Stephanie) Ina Roland, daughter of **George Roland** and the former Frankie Craig; graduate of Texas Southern University.

*Pearl Roland** (b. Nov. 1, 1898; d. Feb. 3, 1970) daughter of **John Pinckney Neely** and the former Missie Pinson; married George E. Roland, the father of two of her children: Mozel and George Robert; also the mother of Vivian Neely Sullivan.

Mooriah Rowser (b. Aug. 5, 1994) daughter of the former **Paula Townsend** and **Morris Rowser**.

Paula Rowser (b. July 4, 1965) daughter of the former **Lillian Maude Fuller** and Wade **Townsend**; married Morris Rowser, the father of her daughter, Mooriah; an x-ray technician, she graduated from South Central Junior College.

Children of the Sputnik Era

In 1957, Russia shocked the world with the launching of Sputnik, the first satell[...] United States reacted with chagrin and the race to the moon[...] How has all this [...] today's children, the children of the age? In the following essays, written for This [...] Washington youngsters who were born in the year of Sputnik discuss the significan[...] Apollo 11 mission.

How I Feel About the Moon Shot

I think the moonshot represents great progress in science and in space research. I think it could help man in many ways.

But one thing is wrong it is alright for them to do research and other projects about the moon but I think it isn't all that much important. It is important but the government should think about all that money that they are spending for it every year. With the many problems in the country, And spending alot of money in Vietnam, plus the millions of dollars use for space Research every year is alot of money.

I think the space program should get up a money raising program and the government should start helping some of the riot torned areas a little more. But still give money to the space research.

The space program is a great project for children like me. But man might never be able to live on the moon. And all that money would be wasted just to risk a mans life although he is Volunteering to do it just to find out Where it came from and other things. And it isn't hardly worth it. But if man could live on the moon it would be great. But we should think about the Planet Earth and all its problems which need money.

The competition race between the United States and Russia is a good one. But I really hope we win because if Russia gets up there before we do we might have a more trouble than we've ever dreamed of. And that's a pretty good reason for us trying to land on the moon.

One suggestion made by me alone is for them to raise money by having a Space boys club where they can learn about space and learn about rockets and be able to build there own little rockets and make books about them and if it succeeds they could earn millions of dollars every year by building them all over

Lawrence Satterfield

the country then the government could pay attention to other problems and wouldn't have to give That much money to the Space research because very dollar counts.

Lawrence Satterfield, age 11
Son of Mr. and Mrs. Lee A. Satterfield
5145 7th St. NE

Lawrence Satterfield (b. Oct. 23, 1957) son of the former **Lorena Herron** and Lee **Satterfield,** Sr. (a lawyer); attended Boston University; vice president, sales, Nortel Communication.

Judge Lee Furman Satterfield (b. Dec. 17, 1958) son of the former **Lorena Herron** and Lee **Satterfield,** Sr. (a lawyer); Appointed to the District of Columbia Superior Court by President George Bush; Began college at Brandeis, before a grave illness forced him to transfer to the University of Maryland; He went on to graduate from the George Washington University National Law Center, served as a trial attorney in the organized crime and racketeering section of the U.S. Department of Justice, and also, as an Assistant U.S. Attorney for the District of Columbia; he married the former Pamela Stever, an assistant U.S. attorney and the mother of his son, Nicholas.

1992, Judge Lee Satterfield and his parents on the day he was sworn in

Lorena Satterfield (b. Sept. 9, 1935) daughter of the former **Edgenora Neely** and Furman **Herron;** married Lee Satterfield (a lawyer who graduated from Howard University's law school) the father of her three children: Lawrence, Lee, and Lori; resident in Washington, D.C..

Lori Satterfield (b. July 12, 1967) daughter of the former **Lorena** Herron and Lee **Satterfield,** Sr. (a lawyer); married; one daughter named Ashley Satterfield-Reid and a son named Aaron Haskel Young.

Nicholas Satterfield (b. May 13, 1995) son of the former Pamela Stever (a lawyer) and **Judge Lee F. Satterfield.**

Amelia Delaine Sheard (b. June 1, 1967) is the daughter of the former **Johnnie Mae** Anderson and

Willie Lee **Boyd;** she attended Benedict College; is married to Mark Sheard; and is the mother of Aurelia Shantell Boyd and Markus Anthony Sheard. Amelia and her family reside in Hodges, S.C..

Markus Anthony Sheard (b. Oct. 27, 1991) son of the former **Amelia Delaine** Boyd and Mark **Sheard**.

Hattie Shell, daughter of the former **Lydie Neely** and Cade **Sullivan**; married Allen Shell (deceased) the father of her five sons and a daughter.

***Sandra Lee Neely Smith** (b. Dec. 25, 1950; d. Nov. 3, 1979) daughter of **Smith W. Neely** and the former Leola Gladden; she married Mark D. Smith. Sandra was a political activist, and her murder during a demonstration in Greensboro, N.C. was reported in the national press.

Sandra Neely Smith

Cade Thomas Sullivan, son of the former **Lydie Neely** and C.T. **Sullivan**.

David Sullivan (b. Apr. 15, 1959) son of **Eddie Pearl Sullivan**.

Eddie Pearl Sullivan (b. Jan. 13, 1924) daughter of the former **Lydie Neely** and Cade **Sullivan**; three sons, Michael, David, and Thomas, and a daughter, Peggy (Young); resides in Washington, D.C..

Homer Lee Sullivan, son of the former **Lydie Neely** and Cade **Sullivan**; married the former Shirley Rollins (who was previously married to Mr. Moore); one daughter.

Joyce Sullivan, daughter of **Alfonzo Neely** and the former Beatrice LaBoon.

Michael Sullivan (b. Jan. 21, 1958) son of **Eddie Pearl Sullivan**, father of Reggie, Randy, and Sheryl.

Lee Sullivan, son of the former **Lydie Neely** and Cade **Sullivan**; married the former Ethel Brown, the mother of his six children: Virginia (Chapman); Lorraine (McDonald); Evetter (Culcleasure); Leroy, Jr.; Lou (Lewers); and Jacqueline (Anderson).

Lee Sullivan, Jr., son of **Leroy Sullivan** and the former Ethel Brown.

*****Lydie Sullivan**, a daughter of **Richard Neely, Sr.**, and the former Harriet Dial Neely; married Cade Thomas ("C.T.") Sullivan,[77] father of her eight children: Flora (Brown); Jessie (Byrd); Hattie (Shell); Eddie Pearl; Leroy; Homer Lee; Plummer; and Cade Thomas.

Lydie Sullivan

---

[77] C.T. Sullivan was the son of T.T. Sullivan and had a half-brother named T.R. Neely.

From left: Cade Sullivan, Plummer Sullivan, and two of their nephews

The sons of the former Lydie Neely and Cade Sullivan: Leroy Sullivan (standing) Homer Sullivan, son-in-law, Ezell Byrd, and Plummer Sullivan

Plummer Sullivan, son of the former **Lydie Neely** and Cade **Sullivan;** married Gladys, mother of his daughter and three sons.

Randy Sullivan, son of **Michael Sullivan.**

Reggie Sullivan, son of **Michael Sullivan.**

Sheryl Sullivan, daughter of **Michael Sullivan.**

Thomas Sullivan (b. Aug. 29, 1948) son of **Eddie Pearl Sullivan;** married the former Dorothy Jackson; one stepdaughter named Jacqueline Queen.

Lydia Sweeney (b. May 16, 1952) daughter of the former **Flora Sullivan** (now, **Harris**); married Harley Sweeney (a member of the same family as Joe W. Sweeney, who married a Pinson cousin—see the footnote under John Pinckney Neely's entry), the father of her daughters, Natalie and Shanetta.

Natalie Sweeney, the daughter of the former **Lydia** Brown and Harley **Sweeney.**

Shanetta Sweeney, the daughter of the former **Lydia** Brown and Harley **Sweeney**.

Maurice Taylor, son of the former **Maude** Neely and Moses **Taylor**.

Maude Hattie Taylor, daughter of **Richard Neely, Jr.** and the former **Beulah Garrett** (see "Cleveland"); married Moses Taylor, the father of her daughter, Myrtle, and son Maurice; also the mother of Frances Alberta Bradley.

Myrtle Taylor (b. Jan. 11, 1940) daughter of the former **Maude Neely** and Moses **Taylor;** she is a processing technician at the Library of Congress and a Poet; she is listed in *Our World's Favorite Poems - Who's Who In Poetry*, has won several Golden and Silver Poet Awards at the Southwest Festival of Arts, been written up in *The Hillrag* and *Southwester* newspapers, recited poetry on WOOK Radio, appeared in commercials for the American Poetry Association and Paragon Needlecraft, and has an article on Clara Barton in the Archives at the Red Cross; As of 1988, she had 17 published poems, including one that appeared in *The American Poetry Anthology*, vol. VII, no. 4, edited by John Frost (Santa Cruz, California.: American Poetry Association, 1987); In 1986, she recited several of her poems at a gathering in the Poetry Room of the Library of Congress, at the invitation of the 1985-86 poetry consultant, Gwendolyn Brooks! She attended Cortez Peters Business College and took writing courses at the Catholic University Adult Center and Trinity College; she is a lifelong resident of Washington, D.C., where she was born.

Rema Thomas (b. Feb. 26, 1975) daughter of **Regina Neely** and her first husband, Elmino Thomas; now attending Temple University.

*****Helen Neely Thompson** daughter of **Walter Neely** and the former **Etta Garlington;** married James Thompson.

Debra Tolbert, daughter of **Otis T. Neely** and Mary; married Johnny Tolbert.

Lillian Maude Fuller Townsend [78] (b. July 22, 1938) daughter of **Houston Neely** and Ollie Mae Coleman Fuller; married Wade Townsend,[79] the father of her four children: Rodney Wade and three daughters: Stephanie, Paula (Rowser) and Dierdre (Johnson); received a masters degree in social work from the University of Connecticut; resides in Connecticut.

(Wade) Rodney Townsend (b. Jan. 16, 1960) son of the former **Lillian Maude** Fuller and Wade **Townsend;** married the former Tanya Valeriano, the mother of his son, Wade Austin; graduated from the University of New Haven in West Haven, Conn.; resides in Md..

Stephanie Townsend (b. Mar. 8, 1958) daughter of the former **Lillian Maude** Fuller and Wade **Townsend;** graduated from South Central Junior College.

---

[78] Lillian Maude is a niece of Alfred Lavon Coleman, listed above under Garretts, the half-brother of her mother.
[79] Wade Townsend's father was Leroy Townsend.

Fosalee Williams

*At the 1992 GNS Reunion in Detroit, MI:
from left, Lee Satterfield, Sr., Raymond Crosson, Jr.,
Furman Herron, Javan Boston, Jr.,
Bessie Crosson, & Lorena Satterfield*

Wade Austin Townsend, the son of **(Wade) Rodney Townsend** and the former Tanya Valeriano.

Mary L. Whinen, daughter of the former **Maggie Sullivan** and the Rev. **Berry Franklin Neely**; married.

Fosalee Maggie Williams, daughter of the former **Maggie Sullivan** and the Rev. **Berry Franklin Neely**; married.

Ollie Yarbrough, daughter of **Calvin Neely** and the former Ollie Cleveland married Booker T. Yarbrough, the father of her seven children: Mary Ellen, Eddie Calvin, Booker, Jr., Frances, Norma (Green) Ethel (Montgomery) and Willie James; resident of Cleveland. Ohio.

Aaron Haskel Young (b. Aug. 11, 1995) the son of **Lori Satterfield**.

Craig Young, son of **Peggy Young**.

Peggy Young (b. October 4, 1949) daughter of **Eddie Pearl Sullivan**; mother of Craig, Tia, and Maya.

Maya Young, daughter of **Peggy Young**.

Tia Young, daughter of **Peggy Young**.

1983: Mrs. Perry Sullivan, II (Ann); Thelma Jeter, Leroy Sullivan, and Perry Sullivan, II

Booker Yarbrough, Jr. son of the former **Ollie Neely** and Booker, Sr., **Yarbrough;** married [Pamela or Catherine?]; resident of Cleveland, Ohio.

Mary Ellen Yarbrough daughter of the former **Ollie Neely** and Booker **Yarbrough**; lives in Cleveland, Ohio.

THE NEELY FAMILY AT THE 1992 GNS REUNION IN DETROIT, MI., INCLUDING GARRETT/NEELYS AND SULLIVAN/NEELYS

THE SULLIVANS

"And also of the son of the bondwoman will I make a nation."
Genesis, 21:13

Haily Sullivan

Haily Sullivan[80] was born in 1815 in South Carolina; she was the mother of Lue (Garlington) and Perry, I. The grandchildren of this slave woman were early graduates of historically Black colleges such as Spellman, Johnson C. Smith, and Tuskegee, and her descendants include two medical doctors (Sylvia Alfreda Merchant and Tonni Sullivan Jones) and many educators (including Searight Sullivan, Mary Humbert, Altamease Culver, and Arnold Sullivan).

Relationship To The Garrett And Neely Families

The former Frances Latimer, wife of Wister Lee Garrett, was the sister of Emma L. Irby, [81] the maternal grandmother of Searight Sullivan's children by his second wife, Fannie; thus, Wick Garrett's children were first cousins to Searight's children by Fannie. Maggie Sullivan, the sister of Searight Sullivan, married Berry Franklin Neely, a son of Richard Neely, Sr. and the former Harriet Dial. Also, Etta Garlington, a grandchild of Haily

Haily Sullivan

---

80 Materials regarding The Sullivans were compiled by Perry Sullivan, II, the son of Searight Sullivan (the third child of Perry, I and Harriet Sullivan) and Arthuree Alberta McCoy, the daughter of Searight's sister, Maggie. LaBrenda Garrett-Nelson supplemented this compilation, based on information from Altamease Culver, the sister of Perry, II, and obituaries provided by Ethel Price and Linda Kumi.

81 Emma Irby was also the mother of Henry Arnold; the father of her children was a Native American who "came from" a reservation (SOURCE: Altamease Sullivan Culver).

Sullivan (and Maggie and Searight Sullivan's first cousin) married Walter Neely, another son of Richard Neely and the former Harriet Dial.

The ties that bind these families go beyond mere legal relationships. Emma Irby lived for a time on Wick Garrett's plantation, and so her Sullivan grandchildren have childhood memories of visiting that place (Perry Sullivan, II, in particular, remembers being fascinated by the fact that Wick and Frances's kitchen was housed in a separate structure that was connected to the main house). When Searight and Fannie Sullivan moved their family to Tampa Florida in 1925; they were joined by Thomas Garrett, the son of Wick Lee Garrett and the former Francis Latimer. Mary Anne Gadson and her brother, Kenneth Franklin (both of whom are listed under "Neelys") remain close to the children of Searight Sullivan who are living in Tampa, Florida. In 1989, Sullivans hosted the GNS reunion in Tampa, and another branch of the Sullivans hosted the 1992 reunion in Detroit.

Lue Garlington

Lue Garlington (b. 1855) was the daughter of Haily Sullivan. She married Smith Garlington (b. 1853); their children were: Emma, Ida, and Etta.

Etta Neely, the daughter of the former **Lue Sullivan** and Smith **Garlington**; married **Walter Neely,** the father of her seven children (see Walter Neely's entry for the names of their children).

Perry Sullivan, I

Perry Sullivan, I (b. 1852, d. 1934) was the son of Haily Sullivan. He had three wives: the former Harriet Young; Martha; and the former Louise Jeter. Perry and Harriet Young had seven children: Willie; Mary (Humbert); Searight; **Maggie Florence** (b. Dec. 26, 1879; d. Dec. 17, 1958, married the Reverend **Berry Franklin Neely;** see his entry for the names of their children); Oscar; Thomas; and Conway; an eighth child, James, died in infancy. Both Searight and Maggie Sullivan Neely attended the 1899-1900 term of the Brainard Institute in Chester, S.C., and their families have a class portrait of that class.

Willie Sullivan (b. Sept. 10, 1872) the first child of **Perry Sullivan,** I and the former Harriet Young; married Minnie; they had no children.

Mary Humbert (b. Nov. 16, 1874) the second child of **Perry Sullivan,** I and the former Harriet Young; married Thomas ("Tom") Humbert, producing three children: Seabrook; Gettis; and Sullivan; she graduated from Spellman College in Atlanta, Ga., and was a public school teacher.

Mary Sullivan Humbert

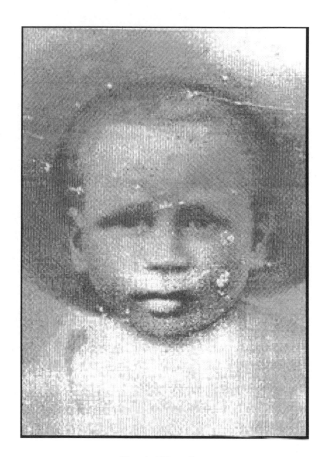

Gettis Humbert

Searight Sullivan (b. Sept. 2, 1876) the third child of **Perry Sullivan**, I and the former Harriet Young; attended Tuskegee. He married twice. The first marriage to Emma Paden Sullivan produced five children: Geneva, Evera, Bernice, and Odessa (Webster) (the youngest was a son who passed in infancy). The second marriage was to the former Fannie Arnold; Fannie was one of his students; the children of this marriage were: Levo (Oliver, Fannie's natural daughter who was adopted by Searight); Emogen (Stubbs); Perry, II; Altamease (Culver); and Arnold (two daughters passed in infancy).

Emma Irby

Fannie Mae Arnold Sullivan

Henry Arnold

Perry Sullivan, I

Oscar Sullivan (b. Aug. 6, 1882) the fifth child of Perry Sullivan and the former Harriet Young; married Fraizer, and had four children: Ira, a daughter; Nathaniel; Minus; and Otis.

Thomas Sullivan (b. Aug 23, 1884) sixth child of Perry Sullivan, I and the former Harriet Young. Ethel Price (listed under Neelys) has a degree, granted on June 8, 1904, from Biddle University in Charlotte, N.C., to T.Y. Sullivan, believed to be Thomas.

Conway Sullivan (b. July 25, 1886) the youngest child of Perry Sullivan and the former Harriet Young; married Maggie, the mother of his two children: Inez and J.T.; J.T. was the parent of a grandchild: Thomas.

Other descendants of Haily Sullivan are:

Fannie Mae Anderson, daughter of **Levo Oliver;** graduated from Temple University, in Philadelphia, Penn.; mother of Carol, Donald, James, Mark, George, and Cheryl.

Carol Anderson, daughter of **Fannie Mae Anderson;** resident of Charlotte, N.C..

Cheryl Anderson, daughter of **Fannie Mae Anderson.**

Dominique Anderson. grandchild of Fannie Mae Anderson.

Donald Anderson, son of **Fannie Mae Anderson.**

George Anderson, son of **Fannie Mae Anderson.**

James Anderson, son of **Fannie Mae Anderson.**

Kalethia Anderson, grandchild of Fannie Mae Anderson.

Mark Anderson, son of **Fannie Mae Anderson.**

Tamika Anderson (b. 1980), grandchild of Fannie Mae Anderson.

*****Rudolph Arnold** (deceased) son of **Levo Oliver.**

Sheriee Bacoat, daughter of **Dr. Tonni Yvonne Bacoat Jones** and Isaac Earl Bacoat.

Thor Ali-Sharif Booker, son of **Dr. Sylvia Alfreda Merchant, M.D.** and her former husband, Robert Booker.

*****Louise Bowie** (d. Jan. 1, 1995) daughter of the former **Ira Sullivan** and Mr. **Redmond.**

Irene Coates, daughter of the former **Ira** Sullivan and Oscar **Redmond.**

Frances Cox, daughter of **Searight Sullivan, II** and Ellen, attended University of South Florida; married Tony Cox[82] (Tony Cox attended the same college).

Altamease Culver (b. Feb. 25, 1927) daughter of **Searight Sullivan** and the former Fannie Arnold; born in Tampa, Florida; her second marriage was to Paul Culver; no children; both she and her husband obtained Masters degrees from Florida A&M University, and both were classroom teachers. Altamease entered college at the age of 16 and graduated at the age of 20! Altamease organized the 1988 family reunion held in Tampa, Florida.

---

[82] Tony Cox was the son of James and Dorothy Cox of Nassau, Bahamas.

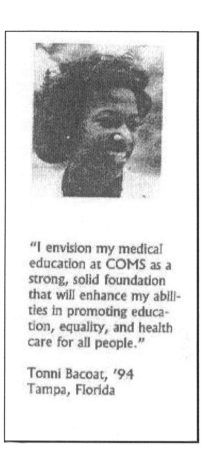

"I envision my medical education at COMS as a strong, solid foundation that will enhance my abilities in promoting education, equality, and health care for all people."

Tonni Bacoat, '94
Tampa, Florida

From Tonni's Medical School Catalogue

Altamease Sullivan Culver

Irene Sullivan Hamilton, daughter of **Minus Sullivan**; married; resides in Tampa, Florida.

*****Gettis Humbert**, youngest son of the former **Mary Sullivan** and Thomas **Humbert**.

*****Seabrook Humbert**, oldest son of the former **Mary Sullivan** and Thomas **Humbert**.

*****Sullivan Humbert**, the middle son of the former **Mary Sullivan** and Thomas **Humbert**; he made a career of military service in the army.

Cameron Jamal Jones (b. December 1994) son of **Dr. Tonni Yvonne Sullivan Jones, M.D.** and Charles Jones.

Dr. Tonni Yvonne Sullivan Bacoat Jones, M.D. (b. Nov. 12, 1960) daughter of **Perry Sullivan, II** and the Birdie; attended Bennett College, in Greensboro, N. C.; graduated from the University of Osteopathic Medicine and Surgery in 1994; first married Ltd. Isaac Earl Bacoat; second marriage to Charles Jones; two children: a daughter, Sheriee Bacoat and a son, Cameron Jamal Jones.

Dr. Sylvia Alfreda Merchant, M.D., daughter of the former **Odessa Sullivan and David Lee Webster**; mother of Thor Ali-Sharif Booker, she graduated from the University of Michigan and later earned a masters degree in French literature from Temple University, before going on to graduate from the University of Osteopathic Medicine and Surgery. She wed Robert Booker on June 8, 1973.

Billie E. Oliver, daughter of **Levo Oliver**; graduated from Wayne State University in Detroit Michigan.

Levo Oliver

Brenda Oliver, daughter of **Levo** and William **Oliver**.

Carolyn Ann Oliver, daughter **of Levo** and William **Oliver**; mother of Kimberly.

Levo Oliver (b. Dec. 30, 1910, Laurens, S.C.) daughter of Searight and **Fannie Arnold Sullivan**, attended South Carolina State College; school teacher; married William Oliver; eight children: Bennie, Fannie Mae, Rudolph (deceased) Thomasena (Washington) Brenda, Carolyn, Cloretta (Stokes) and Billie.

Thomasena Oliver-Washington, daughter of **Levo** and William **Oliver**; mother of Tonya L., Damon K., Tiffany D, and Raphael A..

Ira Redmond, daughter of **Oscar Sullivan** and Fraizer; married Oscar Redmond; the mother of four daughters: Louise (Bowie); Pauline, Alberta, and Irene (Coates); resides in Miami, Fl.

Cloretta Stokes, daughter of **Levo Oliver**; mother of William Lamont.

William Lamont Stokes, son of **Cloretta Stokes.**

Emogene Stubbs (b. May 24, 1917, Laurens, S.C.) daughter of **Searight Sullivan**; and the former Fannie Arnold; married James Stubbs, the father of her daughter, Sherryl (Wilkins); attended Morris College; worked for the Detroit school system in Michigan.

Alden Sullivan (b. March 1956) child of **Arnold Sullivan** and Minnie; married Doris; attended Mercer University, in Macon, Georgia.

Arnold Sullivan (b. Feb. 10, 1933) son of **Searight Sullivan** and the former Fannie Arnold born in Tampa, Florida; one child: Alden; married to Minnie; both he and his wife graduated from Florida A&M where he was a football star; a four-year letterman, he earned SIAC honors in 1953 and 1954, while serving as team captain as a senior on the Rattlers 1953 championship team. He was also tabbed the most understanding senior in the 1954 Orange Blossom Classic; in 1995, he was inducted into the Florida A&M Hall of Fame as a student athlete; a retired classroom teacher and football coach, he resides in Tampa, Florida.

Arnold Sullivan Football 1951-54

From the Florida A&M University Sports Hall of Fame Induction Ceremonies Program

Perry Sullivan, II

Bernice Sullivan (b. Laurens, S.C.) daughter of **Searight Sullivan**, and the former Emma Paden; no children.

*Evera Sullivan (b. Laurens, S.C.; d.) daughter of **Searight Sullivan** and the former Emma Paden; three children: Searight, II; Nathaniel (deceased); and Tova (deceased).

*Geneva Sullivan (b. Laurens, S.C.; d.) daughter of **Searight** and **Sullivan** and the former Emma Paden; born in Laurens, S.C.; the oldest of Searight's children; no children.

J.T. Sullivan, child of **Conway Sullivan** and Maggie; parent of Thomas.

Mary Ellen Sullivan, daughter of **Searight Sullivan, II** and Mary Ellen; resident of Tampa, Fl.

Minus Sullivan, son of **Oscar Sullivan**; father of Irene (Hamilton).

Perry Sullivan, II (b. Aug. 24, 1920, Laurens, S.C.) son of **Searight Sullivan** and the former Fannie Arnold; graduated from Morehouse College, in Atlanta, Ga.; further study at Tulane University; high school classroom teacher; two children from first marriage to Birdie: Perry, III and Tonni Yvonne (Jones); second marriage to the former Ann Smith; Perry retired as a supervisor of a Social and Rehabilitative Service Unit, part of the Health and Rehabilitative Services for the state of Florida. Perry, II was one of about 300 who fought in the Army's 394th anti-aircraft battalion during World War II

*Tova Sullivan, child of **Evera Sullivan**, parent of Clarence, Sheila (mother of Donald) Tyrone, Leon, and Eric.

Thomas Sullivan, child of **J.T. Sullivan**.

*Bennie Thompson (d. 1995) son of **Levo Oliver**; married Judie; father of Lisa; resident of Dyer, Tenn.

Lisa Thompson, daughter of **Bennie Thompson** and Judie.

Damon K. Washington, son of **Thomasena Washington**.

Raphael A. Washington, Jr., son of **Raphael A. Washington, Sr..**

Raphael A. Washington, Sr., son of the former **Thomasena Washington**.

Tiffany D. Washington, daughter of Thomasena Washington.

Tonya L. Washington, daughter of **Thomasena Washington**.

Noel Webster, son of the former **Odessa Sullivan** and David Lee **Webster**.

*Odessa Sullivan Webster (b. Jan. 21, 1910; Laurens, S.C.; d. 1979) daughter of **Searight Sullivan** and the former Emma Paden; married David Lee Webster, the father of her son, Noel G., and daughter, Sylvia (Merchant); she was a self-employed beautician who lived in Tampa, Fl., for 54 years[84].

Perry Sullivan, III (b. Feb. 24, 1956) son of **Perry Sullivan, II** and Birdie; married and divorced Margie Glen[83] graduated from Florida A&M University; architect.

Searight Sullivan, II, son of **Evera Sullivan**; married Mary Ellen, father of Sandra (mother of Alexander) Susan (mother of Franklin and Darrel) Frances (Cox) and Mary Ellen.

---

[83] Margie Glen was a teacher who was the daughter of Mrs. Janie Lee Glen of Tampa and the late Edgar Glen.

[84] SOURCE: Obituary of Odessa Sullivan Webster

Odessa Sullivan Webster

Smith W. Neely (listed under Neelys) a great-grandson of Haily Sullivan

Darius Wilkins, son of **Sherryl Wilkins**.

Jeremy Wilkins, son of **Sherryl Wilkins**.

Sherryl Wilkins, daughter of the former **Emogene Sullivan** and Mr. **Stubbs** graduated from Wayne State in Detroit; systems engineer for IBM; two children: Jeremy and Darius; resident of Roswell, Ga.

Altamease Sullivan Culver in 1943

COLLEGES AND UNIVERSITIES ATTENDED BY MEMBERS OF THE GARRETT, NEELY, AND SULLIVAN FAMILIES

Following in the footsteps of men such as John Pinckney Neely, who focused on sending his daughters to college because he believed that his sons would have an easier time supporting themselves, Perry Sullivan, II, a "Morehouse Man," and Casper George Garrett, of whom it was written that he "reared a big family of intelligent children who have been given the best educational advantage,"[85] we have always nurtured a love for learning and praised the talented among us.[86]

Adelphi University, New York
Linda McCoy Kumi

Allen University, South Carolina
Lucius Warren Dakers (long-time president of Alumni Association)
Alice Garrett (wife of Bobby Fletcher Garrett)

Casper George Garrett (the first college graduate, lawyer, newspaper publisher, and college professor in the Garrett family)
Christopher Threewitts Garrett, Jr.
John Wesley Garrett (1926 graduate)
Mattie Phyllis (Garrett) Simons (first female graduate of the College Department)

American University, Washington, D.C.
Elaine Simons (wife of William H. Simons, Masters)

Atlanta College of Mortuary Science
Marion Beasley

Atlanta University, Georgia
Naiomi Mills Garrett (Masters)

Bank Street College, New York
Arthuree Neely McCoy

Barber Scotia College
Akousua Korantema Ree Kumi

---

[85] History of the American Negro, p. 319.
[86] Unless otherwise noted, the listed individuals pursued an undergraduate degree.

Baylor University, Texas
John Dakers

Benedict College in Columbia, S.C.
Kathryn Barksdale (bachelors)
Betty McDowell Beasley (wife of Willie L. Beasley)
Naiomi Mills Garrett (bachelors)
Marjorie Johnson
Shelly Ruth Kimpson (bachelors)
The Rev. David Kennedy (bachelors)
Lila Garrett Lloyd (bachelors)
Mamie Lee Beasley Lynch
Wilfred Garrett Rogers (bachelors)
Alfred Simons, Sr. (husband of Mattie Phyllis Simons)
Amelia Boyd Sheard

Bennett College, North Carolina
Dr. Tonni Yvonne Sullivan Bacoat Jones, M.D.

Berkeley, California
Jocelyn Ferguson (Masters and a Ph. D.)

Boston University
Lawrence Satterfield

Bowie State University
William Penn Lloyd (Masters)
Akousua Korantema Ree Kumi
Brandeis
Judge Lee F. Satterfield

Brooklyn Polytech
Leslie Hall-Garrett (Masters, wife of Thomas Weldon Garrett, Jr.)

Brown University, Rhode Island
Alexis Garrett Stodghill (bachelors)

Catholic University, Washington, D.C.
Christopher Threewitts Garrett, III (Masters)
Myrtle Taylor

City University of New York
Denise (Garrett) Fredericks (Bronx Community College and City College)

Madeline Gamble (Queens College)
Thomas Weldon Garrett, Jr. (bachelors, Hunter College and Medgar Evers College)
Tony Grayson (Queens College)
Jeffrey Grayson (Medgar Evers College)
Richard Juan Neely (City College)
LaBrenda Garrett-Nelson (bachelors, John Jay College of Criminal Justice)
Arthuree Neely McCoy (Hunter College)
Denise Worrell-Garrett (bachelors, Bernard Barauch) (wife of Albert Elton Garrett, II)
Leslie Garrett (Medgar Evers) (Associates, wife of Thomas Weldon Garrett, Jr.)
Kumba Creary (step-granddaughter of Thomas Weldon Garrett, Sr., Brooklyn College)
Jacqueline McKinnon (stepdaughter of Thomas Weldon Garrett, Sr., City College)

Clark, Georgia
Cora Altamease Lyons

Clemson University, South Carolina
Richard Charles Garrett ((Masters)
Diane Hansford
Ogden Hansford, Sr. (husband of Diane Hansford)
Alma Lisa McDuffie
Robin Kimiko McDuffie

College of Charleston
Julius Gus Beasley

Columbia University
Naiomi Mills Garrett (Ph. D.)
Dr. Alfred Edgar Simons (D. Ed.)

Columbia Pacific University
Lila Garrett Lloyd (Ph. D.)

Columbia Junior College, South Carolina
Anjanette D. Boyd

Cortez Peters Business College
Myrtle Taylor

Elon College, North Carolina

Marsha (nee Hughes) Grayson (bachelors, wife of the Rev. Glenn Grayson)

Fashion Institute of Technology

Kumba Creary (step-granddaughter of Thomas Weldon Garrett, Sr.)

Fisk University

Linda McCoy Kumi

Fordham University, New York

Alice J. Garrett (wife of Bobby Fletcher Garrett, Masters)

Florida A&M

Altamease Sullivan Culver (Masters)
Paul Culver (husband of Altamease Sullivan, Masters)
Nicole Gadson
Robert Gadson
Cora Altamease Lyons
Murray Lee Neely
Arnold Sullivan
Minnie Sullivan (wife of Arnold Sullivan)
Perry Sullivan, III

Florida State

John Dakers

Georgia Tech

Wilma Lorraine Simons (M.B.A.)

Georgetown University

William Nicholson (J.D.)
Wilma Lorraine Simons

George Washington University

Kwami Kumi (husband of Linda McCoy Kumi)
Josephine Monica Nicholson (Masters)
Judge Lee F. Satterfield (J.D.)

Hampton University

Simone Kay Beasley
Nya Khus Creary (step-grandson of Thomas Weldon Garrett, Sr.)

Haverford College

David Nicholson

Hood Theological Seminary

The Rev. Glenn Garrett Grayson (Masters)

Hofstra University

Michelle Martin

Howard University

Demetrius Coleman
Phyllis Threewitts Ferguson
Marjorie Johnson (graduate work)
Veronica Jordan
Linda McCoy Kumi (Masters)
Ruth Simons Nicholson
Garrett Ridgley
Lee Satterfield, Sr. (husband of Lorena Satterfield, Law Degree)
Kemble Taylor Simons

(Colored Normal) Industrial Agricultural Memorial College of South Carolina

Hattie Garrett (1908 graduate)

Indiana University

Clifton H. Lloyd, Sr. (husband of Lila Garrett Lloyd)

University of Iowa

David Nicholson (Masters)

Johnson C. Smith College (formerly, Biddle University) Charlotte, N.C.

John Nathan Boston
Barbara Graden (wife of Richard Garrett)
Carolyn Beasley Shortt
Robert Elisha Shortt (husband of Carolyn Shortt)
T.Y. Sullivan (1904 graduate of Biddle)

Lander University (formerly, College) South Carolina

Calvin Leon Goodwin (husband of Shelby Ananie Goodwin)
Bobbinetta Lander (bachelors)
Marye Elaine Hunter (bachelors)

Janet (Presley) Kennedy (bachelors, wife of the Rev. David Kennedy)

Lincoln University
Colon Hunter Garrett
Kwabena Debiate Lee Kumi

Livingston College at Rutgers
Dierdre Elaine Townsend Johnson

Livingstone College, North Carolina
The Rev. Glenn Garrett Grayson (bachelors)
Cavernetta Beasley
Wanda Priscilla Denny
Ronnie Grayson

Meharry Dental School
Dr. Colon Hunter Garrett (1927 graduate)

Mercer University, Macon, Ga.
Alden Sullivan

Michigan State
Delrico Simons

Miner Teachers College
Dr. Alfred E. Simons, Jr.
William H. Simons
Elaine Simons (wife of William H. Simons)
Josephine Simons Wade
Mills McDaniel Simons

Montgomery College
Akousa Korantema Kumi

Morehouse College
Perry Sullivan, II
Charles Derrick Stodghill (father of Alexis Garrett Stodghill)

Morgan State University
Garey Crosson
Greg Grayson

Morris College
Arthuree Neely McCoy
Inona McRae

Cora Estella Neely
Willie Blanch Neely
Emogene Stubbs

National University, Sacramento, Ca.
Raymond Allan McCoy

New York University
LaBrenda Garrett-Nelson (J.D.; LL.M.)
Marjorie Johnson (graduate work)
Sheryl Patrice Simons
Josephine Simons Wade (Masters)
Nia Endesha Halima Williams
Charles Derrick Stodghill (J.D., (father of Alexis Garrett Stodghill)

NC Central University
Clifton H. Lloyd, Sr. (Masters, husband of Lila Garrett Lloyd)
Greg Curtis Grayson (bachelors)

North Carolina A & T
Chaunte Garrett
Ryan Grayson
William Penn Lloyd (bachelors)
Mary Ann Summers
Demaunt Shannon Robinson

North Carolina College, Durham, N.C.
Dorothy Rose Dakers Smith (bachelors)

North Carolina Central
Greg Grayson

Ohio State University
Murray Lee Neely (Masters of Science)

Park College, Missouri
Paul Anthony Simons

Piedmont Tech
Todd Keith Dakers

Penn State
Nia Endesha Halima Williams

COLLEGES AND UNIVERSITIES ATTENDED...

Presbyterian, Clinton, S.C.
Cornelia Elaine Walker

Sacramento City College
Denise Mason

Sacramento State University
Erma Jean Mason

Sanoma State University
Erina McCoy (bachelors)

Seattle Central College
Jocelyn Ferguson

Seton Hall, New Jersey
Glenn J. Jeter

South Carolina State College
(Wister) Paul Boston
Fletcher Mills Garrett
Marion Threewitts Garrett
Mamie Kennedy
Dr. Ellington Cortez Moore (Masters of Science)
Levo Oliver
Juliet Summers Ware

South Central Junior College, Connecticut
Paula Rowser
Stephanie Townsend

Southern University School of Law
Calvin Leon Goodwin (law degree, husband of Shelby Ananie Goodwin)

Spellman College, Atlanta, Ga.
Mary (Sullivan) Humbert

Springfield College, Massachusetts
Tony Grayson
Rebecca Grayson (wife of Tony Grayson)

Staten Island University
Karen Michelle Dakers

State University of New York
Leslie Garrett (bachelors, wife of Thomas Weldon Garrett, Jr., Empire State)

Thomas Weldon Garrett, Jr. (M.B.A., Empire State)
Kevin Nick Hunter (husband of Marye Elaine Hunter, New Paul)

St. John's University
Danielle Garrett

Syracuse University, New York
Beryl Dakers Burton

Temple University
Fannie Mae Anderson
Raeshawn L. Crosson
Dorothy Rose Dakers Smith
Rema Thomas
Sylvia Webster Merchant (Masters)

Texas Southern University
George Roland
Frankie (Craig) Roland (wife of George Roland)
George Anthony (Tony) Roland
(Stephanie) Ina Roland (bachelors)

Tufts
William Garrett Nicholson (bachelors)

Tulane University
Perry Sullivan, II (graduate work)

Tuskegee
Searight Sullivan
Desmond Gadson

United Brotherhood Technical College of Carpenters & Joiners of America
Eugene Fredericks (husband of Denise Fredericks)

United States Naval Academy (Annapolis)
Jon Myron Simons (1982 graduate)

University of California (Berkley)
Jocelyn Ferguson (Masters and Ph.D.)

University of Chicago
Ruth Simons Nicholson

University of Connecticut
Lillian Maude Townsend (Masters)

University of the District of Columbia
Crystal Bradley
DeCarlos Bradley
Kenneth Crosson
Charrisse Nelson (step-daughter of LaBrenda Garrett-Nelson)
David Nicholson

University of Illinois at Urbana-Champagne
Kwabena Dabiete Leey Kumi (bachelor of science)

University of Maryland,
Linda McCoy Kumi (second bachelors, University College)
Dr. Phyllis Nicholson, M.D. (M.D.)
Judge Lee F. Satterfield

University of Massachusetts
Dr. Ellington Cortez Moore (Ed. D.)

University of Memphis (formerly, Memphis State University)
Sheila Robinson-Beasley (J.D.; wife of Julius Gus Beasley)

University of Michigan
Dr. Sylvia Webster Merchant, M.D.

University of New Haven, Connecticut
Wade Rodney Townsend

University of North Carolina, Chapel Hill
Alice J. Garrett (wife of Bobby Fletcher Garrett, Ph.D.)

University of North Carolina at Greensboro
Lila Garrett Lloyd (Ph.D.)

University of Osteopathic Medicine and Health Sciences
Dr. Tonni Y.S. Bacoat-Jones (M.D.)
Dr. Sylvia Webster Merchant (M.D.)

University of Ottawa, Canada
Kwami Kumi (husband of Linda McCoy Kumi)

University of Pennsylvania, Wharton School of Social Work
Dorothy Rose Dakers Smith (graduate work)

University of Rochester
Phyllis Wade Logan

University of South Carolina
Shelby Ananie Goodwin (Masters)
Abigail Ramona Harris (J.D.)
Wilfred Garrett Rogers (Masters)
Charles Beasley

University of South Florida
Frances M. Sullivan
Desmond Gadson

University of Washington
Jocelyn Ferguson

Vorhees College, South Carolina
Richard Charles Garrett (bachelors)
Nya Khus Creary (step-grandson of Thomas Weldon Garrett, Sr.)

Wagner College, Staten Island, N.Y.
Sharyn Tucker McCalla

Wake Forest, North Carolina
Marsha Grayson (wife of the Rev. Glenn Garrett Grayson, J.D.)

Washington State University
Kay Ferguson

Wayne State University
Billie Oliver
Sherryl Stubbs Wilkins

Roberts Wesleyan
Phyllis Wade Logan

Wilson College, Pennsylvania
Josephine Monica Nicholson

Winthrop College
Shelby Ananie Goodwin (bachelors)

Wofford College
Kenneth Edward Beasley

Yale
Kevin Simons

Others (Those Known to Have Attended Unidentified Institutions)
Jonathan Beasley
Kevin Garrett

Thomas Garrett
Dr. Gerian Steven Moore
Ellen Neely
Regina Neely
Odessa M. Poole
Early Smith

ADDENDUM

GARRETTS

Lauren Alexis Beasley (b. March 23, 1999), daughter of Kenneth and Michelle Crosby Beasley.

Nicole Kennedy wed Julio **Chelviar** on July 8, 2000.

Simone K. Beasley wed Terence L. **Cleveland** on May 22, 1999.

Alfred Lavon Coleman died.

Chase Zekiel Garrett (b. April 4, 2000) son of Lathia Garrett.

Kevin Garrett wed LaDeva Carrington on August 26, 2000.

Dr. Naomi Mills Garrett died on May 30, 2000.

Savannah A. Grayson (b. Feb. 20, 1999) daughter of Dwight and Tenderly Grayson.

Callie Kennedy died on January 7, 2000.

Toure Bicarri Kennedy (b. April 12, 2000) son of Lola Kennedy.

Sandra B. Kennedy wed Roosevelt **Kinaird**, Jr. on September 9, 2000.

DeAndrei Tyshun Leake (b. Aug. 2, 1999) son of Tya L. Kennedy.

Demaunt Shannon Robinson changed his legal name to **Prince El-Khaalik**.

Wilfred Garrett Rogers and his wife became the parents of twin boys, **Winston and Stanton Rodgers**.

Dorothy Dakers Smith died on December 12, 1999.

Alma Summers died on June 24, 1999.

Edward Jordan Tucker, Jr. died on April 5, 1999.

Bobbinetta Garrett wed BF **Young** on May 24, 2000.

NEELYS

LeJani Vanya Goodwin (b. March 4, 1999), child of Jensine and Lemoyne Goodwin.

Audrey C. Everett is the daughter of Robert Nesbitt Neely.

COLLEGES AND UNIVERSITIES

Brooklyn Polytechnic University
Leslie Hall-Garrett (Masters)

Cortez Peters Business College
Valerie Elmore Neely

Frances Marion University
Brittney Burton
Veronica L. Sullivan (bachelors)

Liberty University
Shani C. Anderson

Massey Business College
Ronnie P. Elmore

Newberry College
Albert Elton Garrett, III

Pace University
Rebecca Grayson (wife of Tony Grayson, J.D.)

South Carolina State College
Joyce Elmore Anderson
Victor J. Elmore

University of North Carolina, Chapel Hill
Shaneice McCalla

University of North Carolina, Charlotte
Kontia Grant

Unidentified Institutions
Carolyn Dakers

MISCELLANY

Johnnie Belinda Kennedy's husband, Dr. John H. **Grant** is a cousin to NBA star, Grant Hill.

Alexis Garrett Bowman Stodghill (second from right, below) appeared in a National Magazine Ad campaign with her colleagues from Blackplanet.com, in the Fall of 2000, in a photograph taken by famed photographer Richard Avedon. Also, Beryl Dakers Burton reported that her mother, Lorraine, was also a Bowman from Orangeburg County, SC.

Sandra Lee Neely Smith (article included in first edition of this book reproduced below).

Missing Footnote Citations (from first edition of this book)

1st paragraph on Page 3: *South Carolina, A Guide to the Palmetto State*, p. 47.

1st paragraph on page 5: *Black Slave Owners*, p. 37 and p. 35.

Dublin Hunter was one of only 11 "Free Negro Heads of Families" listed for Laurens County in historian Carter G. Woodson's seminal 1925 study.

1st paragraph on page 11: *The Black Family in Slavery and Freedom*, p. 232.

Page 18: *The Black Family in Slavery and Freedom*, p. 200.

All Six Freed in Klan Murder Trial
In the Deaths of Five Communists

FROM THE NEW YORK TIMES, Nov. 17, 1980: Report of the Acquittal of the Klansmen
Charged With The Death of Sandra Lee Neely Smith

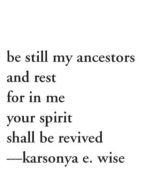

This group of friends took the initiative to start a real life community of websites that would fill th
cultural diversity online. With the help of a dedicated team, they are committed to creating online
communities that offer users a dynamic medium to communicate and interact with those of similar
backgrounds.

So far, their enthusiasm has launched Black Planet.com and Asian Avenue.com. Their next goal is
a community for the Latino market that will empower Latinos. Soon these cultural, political and
entertainment destinations will link us all.

be still my ancestors
and rest
for in me
your spirit
shall be revived
—karsonya e. wise

BIRTHS

MARRIAGES

OTHER MILESTONES

_____

_____

_____

_____

_____

_____

_____

_____

_____

_____

_____

_____

_____

Made in the USA
Columbia, SC
24 January 2022